Leading
SCHOOLS
in a Data-Rich World

Leading SCHOOLS
in a Data-Rich World

Harnessing Data for School Improvement

LORNA M. EARL
STEVEN KATZ

Foreword by Michael Fullan

CORWIN PRESS
A SAGE Publications Company
Thousand Oaks, California

For information:

Corwin Press
A Sage Publications Company
2455 Teller Road
Thousand Oaks, California 91320
www.corwinpress.com

Sage Publications Ltd.
1 Oliver's Yard
55 City Road
London EC1Y 1SP
United Kingdom

Sage Publications India Pvt. Ltd.
B-42, Panchsheel Enclave
Post Box 4109
New Delhi 110 017 India

Printed in the United States of America

Library of Congress Cataloging-in-Publication Data

Earl, Lorna M. (Lorna Maxine), 1948-
Leading schools in a data-rich world: Harnessing data for school improvement / Lorna M. Earl, Steven Katz.
      p. cm.
Includes bibliographical references and index.
ISBN 1–4129–0645–8 (cloth)—ISBN 1–4129–0646–6 (pbk.)
   1. School management and organization. 2. School improvement programs.
3. Educational planning—Statistical methods. I. Katz, Steven. II. Title.
LB2805.E23 2006
371.2—dc22

                                                 2005026850
This book is printed on acid-free paper.

06   07   08   09   10   10 9   8   7   6   5   4   3

Acquisitions Editor:	Rachel Livsey
Editorial Assistant:	Phyllis Cappello
Production Editor:	Melanie Birdsall
Typesetter:	C&M Digitals (P) Ltd.
Copyeditor:	Lynn McBrien
Proofreader:	Mary Meagher
Indexer:	Sheila Bodell
Cover Designer:	Michael Dubowe

Contents

Foreword   vii
    Michael Fullan

About the Authors   ix

Acknowedgments   xi

Introduction   xiii

1. Putting Data at the Center of School Improvement   1
    Awash With Data   1
    Data as a Policy Lever   2
    Educators' Skepticism About Data   3
    Needing to Know   5
    Thinking Differently About Data   7
    Accountability Redefined   9
    Choosing Accountability Through Informed
        Professional Judgment   10
    The Role of Data in Informed Professional Judgment   12
    Using Data to "Take Charge of Change"   14

2. Using Data for Informed Decision Making   17
    An Inquiry Habit of Mind   18
    Data Literacy   18
    A Culture of Inquiry   20
    Leading in a Data-Rich World   22

3. Cultivating the Qualities of Data-Driven Leadership   23
    The Painting Metaphor   23
    Inquiry Habit of Mind   26
    Data Literacy   27
    A Culture of Inquiry   28
    A Gallery Full of Paintings   29

4. Developing an Inquiry Habit of Mind   31
    Setting the Canvas   31
    Planning This Picture   36

5. Becoming Data Literate   45
   Blocking the Canvas   46
   The First Strokes   63

6. Creating a Culture of Inquiry   87
   The Image Grows   87
   Displaying the Picture   96

7. Sustaining the Process: The Cycle of Inquiry   101
   The Next Picture, and the Next, and the Next   108

Resource: Task Sheets for Assignments   **109**

References   **127**

Index   **131**

Foreword

Over the past decade there has been exponential attention paid to accountability, assessment for and of learning, and the glut of information that accompanies such phenomenon, aided and abetted by the fantastic increase in technology. Having reams of data, however, does not by itself make us smarter—only overloaded and confused.

This is where Lorna M. Earl and Steven Katz come in. *Leading Schools in a Data-Rich World* is just what the doctor ordered to make data work for the betterment of schools. *Leading Schools* is simultaneously deep and practical. It puts data at the center but also puts it in perspective. It gives data a purpose and a set of conceptual and strategic tools for using knowledge wisely and effectively.

The authors show us how to use data for informed decision making; moreover, they insist that data must be used to serve continuous inquiry, not just to answer the question of the day. A great strength of *Leading Schools* is the use of an actual case woven through the book, each appearance accompanied by guided assignments which require and enable the reader to go deeper and deeper. We are helped at each step of the way to practice our own inquiry. This is a book that should be read and worked through by teams and groups at the school and district levels. It is a perfect study-group book because it serves as a practical and powerful action plan for continuous improvement.

Earl and Katz have presented a marvelous characterization of today's data-rich world and have helped us take advantage of the great knowledge potential that exists in our computers and heads. Above all, they give purpose to data as they model what a culture of sustained inquiry should become.

—*Michael Fullan*

About the Authors

Lorna M. Earl is Director, Aporia Consulting Ltd., and a recently retired Associate Professor in the Theory and Policy Studies Department and Head of the International Centre for Educational Change at the Ontario Institute for Studies in Education at the University of Toronto (OISE/ UT). Her career has spanned research, policy, and practice in school districts, provincial government, and academe. After 25 years as a Research Officer and Research Director in school districts, she was the first Director of Assessment for the Ontario Education Quality and Accountability Office. Dr. Earl is a teacher and a researcher with a background in psychology and education and a doctorate in Epidemiology and Biostatistics. As a leader in the field of assessment and evaluation, she has been involved in consultation, research, and staff development with teachers' organizations, ministries of education, school boards, and charitable foundations around the world.

Steven Katz is a director with the research and evaluation firm Aporia Consulting Ltd. and a faculty member in Human Development and Applied Psychology at the Ontario Institute for Studies in Education (OISE) of the University of Toronto. He is an associate member of the School of Graduate Studies and is the coordinator of the Psychology of Learning and Development initial teacher education strand.

Dr. Katz holds a doctorate in human development and applied psychology, with a specialization in cognitive science. His areas of expertise include cognition and learning, teacher education, and the design of data-driven systems for organizational accountability, planning, and improvement. He has received the Governor General's medal for excellence in his field and has been involved in research and evaluation, professional development, and consulting with a host of educational organizations around the world.

Acknowledgments

The contributions of the following reviewers are gratefully acknowledged:

James Kelleher
Assistant Superintendent
Scituate Public Schools
Scituate, MA

Edie Holcomb
Executive Director of Instructional Services
Kenosha Unified School District No. 1
Kenosha, WI

Ronald L. Russell
Assessment Consultant
Licensed School Psychologist
Loess Hills Area Education Agency 13
Atlantic, IA

Lesley Anderson
Director, Postgraduate Professional Development
The Open University
Milton Keynes
United Kingdom

Introduction

Each week we receive the *Times Educational Supplement* from England and *Education Week* from the United States. Between us, we also subscribe to several Canadian newspapers, a number of educational journals, and popular magazines from different countries. A quick glance at any of these publications makes it very clear that there is no escaping the presence of data in education. As researchers whose stock in trade is "data," we have become increasingly interested in the role that data have to play in educational change, particularly in how school leaders feel about, understand, and use the mountains of data that are being generated about schools. As we have worked with and talked with educators across the United States, Canada, and around the world, we have been struck by the interest that they show in using data, closely coupled, however, with anxiety and uncertainty.

It is important to start this book by saying that we are data advocates, but we are not data-obsessed. Our interactions over the years with practitioners and leaders in schools have convinced us that data can have a powerful and positive effect on the way decisions are made in schools when they are used as tools for thinking about and planning for change. We are also very cognizant that schools need much more than data to improve. Data form a small but, in our view, essential component of the process of schools becoming functional and valuable players in a knowledge society.

This book, and the workshops that preceded it, emerged from our belief that the real benefits accrue from "getting to know" data as part of an ongoing process of educational change and using it locally to investigate real issues in particular schools as a way of deciding what to do next. We are concerned that schools are being pushed and enslaved by data rather than being steered by leaders, with data providing information that they can use to engage in thoughtful planning and make reasoned and targeted decisions to move towards continuous improvement. Over the years, we have worked with school leaders in a number of jurisdictions, and they have convinced us that they are willing and interested users of data. At the same time, they have told us that they feel uncomfortable with the sheer amount of data that surrounds them and the expectation that they use it.

We hope that *Leading Schools in a Data-Rich World: Harnessing Data for School Improvement* offers images and stimulates possibilities for school leaders who are struggling to cope with the demands and challenges of making data useful rather than burdensome. It is designed to involve school leaders (formal and informal) in using "evidence" of all kinds to bring increased clarity and coherence to the work that they do every day. We even believe that when leaders get comfortable with the ideas and the processes contained in this book and see how using data can move their schools forward, they will become data advocates themselves.

Leading Schools in a Data-Rich World: Harnessing Data for School Improvement is a combination text and workbook that has been designed to provide insights and examples, as well as tasks and challenges. We think of you not as readers but as participants, rolling up your sleeves and digging into the process. It will be messy, frustrating, and demanding; but it will be rewarding.

USING THIS BOOK

We have structured *Leading Schools in a Data-Rich World: Harnessing Data for School Improvement* so that school leaders, school teams, study groups, and graduate classes can use it as a template to engage in interpreting and using data as part of on ongoing planning and refining process. We have organized it first to "tell" you some useful information and theory about using data and then to "show" you with an extended case study of a school using data. Finally, we provide tools for you to "do it" yourself.

Although the book can be read alone, the process depends on people working together to think, argue, and make decisions. We recommend that it be used by teams or groups who are trying to make sense of using data in their own contexts. You will find that the learning occurs in the dissonance and in coming to understand how and what others are thinking.

At the end of this introduction is the first installment of a case example based on a real school, which we develop throughout the book as the process unfolds. There is also the first of a series of assignments for participants to complete as they work through the book. Each chapter includes questions for reflection and discussion by participants. The Resource section includes task sheets that can be photocopied and used by the group. We suggest that planning groups read through the complete text as an introduction to the process and the ideas and then start over, using the questions and the assignments as guides for their own work.

Chapters 1 and 2 contain the rationale and background for our conviction that using data is an essential part of leading and learning in schools. In *Chapter 1: Putting Data at the Center of School Improvement,* we describe the ascendancy of data as an element in educational reform, explore the love/hate relationship that leaders have had with data over the years, and address the thorny issue of accountability. We argue that educators can choose to refocus accountability to connect with their efforts at improvement as they move to informed professional decision making based on evidence. In *Chapter 2: Using Data for Informed Decision Making,* we describe what it will take for school leaders to operate comfortably in a data-rich world by defining a set of leadership capacities related to developing an inquiry habit of mind, becoming data literate, and creating a culture of inquiry in their schools.

Chapters 3, 4, 5, and 6 focus on a process for thinking about data and about how it can inform and challenge the views that educators hold as they plan and implement school improvement activities. *Chapter 3: Cultivating the Qualities of Data-Driven Leadership* offers a metaphor for using data for improvement in which school leaders are likened to artists. Artists are always driven by data—by the colors, textures, and images that they observe, investigate, and respond to. They use their considerable interpretive talent and experience to draw the salient features to the foreground, emphasize important dimensions, and communicate a mood and a message to the audience. This metaphor of school leader as artist offers an alternate view to an image of leaders as automatons, using data to paint by numbers on a canvas designed by someone far away. Leaders are producers of images of their schools and of their educational futures. *Chapter 4: Developing an Inquiry Habit of Mind* incorporates the first two stages in the painting process—*setting the canvas* and *planning the picture.* It details a planning process based on what leaders already know about their schools and where they want to go with them. In it we continue the artistic metaphor to identify the audiences and purposes that will shape the images to come.

In *Chapter 5: Becoming Data Literate* we describe the next two stages in the painting metaphor—*blocking the canvas* and *creating the image.* It includes a process for moving from planning to identifying the necessary indicators (colors on the palette) and locating actual data sources for this picture, and it provides a framework for interpreting and displaying the data to create the images. In this chapter, we explore issues related to the quality of the image (reliability, validity, integrity, ethics, clarity) in practical terms and help the reader to engage with their original purpose of communicating for the intended audiences. Because this chapter contains all of the data that H. C. Andersen school has to review with details about their conversations so that the reader can get the full flavor of the interpretation process, it is a very long chapter. We hope you will persevere.

The real learning comes in grappling with the details of data. *Chapter 6: Creating a Culture of Inquiry* describes a continuous process of using the data for planning next steps by moving from the semi-private world of creating knowledge to the public forum of sharing and distributing knowledge and using the feedback and conversations to define the next stage of improvement. *Chapter 7: Sustaining the Process* describes the ongoing process of inquiry as a habit of practice.

THE CASE EXAMPLE

The following case example comes from our experiences with one school as it has evolved in its orientation towards the use of data. This example will be developed throughout the book to show the challenges, dilemmas, insights, and successes that the school faces along the way.

Janet Chalmers is the newly appointed principal of H. C. Andersen Middle School. The school serves 800 young adolescents (Grades 6–8). It is situated in an "inner suburb" of a mid-sized city (pop. 500,000). The community is largely residential with most students living in bungalows, others in high-rise apartments, and some in a number of townhouse developments that were built in the 1970s. The student body is relatively diverse, with about 20 different ethnic groups represented. In recent years, the population has been somewhat transient as new immigrant families move out to more affluent suburbs and are replaced by other new families.

Janet is excited to be coming to H. C. Andersen. The school has a good reputation for school spirit, and the sports teams do very well in city competitions. Academically, they are not distinguished but have been solid in their performance. For a number of years they have been using a middle school philosophy that focuses on engaging the students in school activities and keeping them excited about school.

The staff at H. C. Andersen is cohesive and committed. There are 32 teachers and 8 support staff, plus custodial workers and several itinerant staff such as a psychologist, speech pathologist, and special education support. Some of the teachers have been there for most of their careers, and others have chosen to come to the school because of its reputation.

Throughout the rest of this book, we will use the H. C. Andersen School as an example of ways in which schools can think about, work with, and use data as a positive force in planning and implementing improvement initiatives.

YOUR ASSIGNMENT

At the same time as we develop the example as an illustration, we have included assignments for you to work with your own data, in your own context. In this first assignment, you are asked to describe your context in enough detail to allow others to imagine what it is like. (Task sheets for use by participants are included in the Resource section.)

Assignment #1

Our School

Use Task Sheet #1 in the Resource section to describe your school. What is your school context? Have all persons in the group privately describe their school as they believe it is seen by others and share their descriptions with one other person in the group. As they share, the pairs should create a composite description, highlighting the similarities and differences in their perceptions. Post the composites on the wall and, as a group, use them to create (1) a description that everyone agrees about and (2) a list of areas of disagreement or uncertainty.

Putting Data at the Center of School Improvement

The premise underlying this book is that data can and should be a compelling force in improving schools. But using data is a relatively new activity in education that is not always a comfortable one for educators, for many reasons. In this chapter, we try to uncover some of the discomfort and develop a set of arguments for why educators should shift their views and think about using data as an essential part of their work.

AWASH WITH DATA

There was a time in education when decisions were based on the best judgments of the people in authority. It was assumed that school leaders, as professionals in the field, had both the responsibility and the right to make decisions about students, schools, and even about education more broadly. They did so using a combination of political savvy, professional training, logical analysis, and intimate and privileged knowledge of the context. Data played almost no part in decisions. In fact, there was not much data available about schools. Instead, leaders relied on their tacit knowledge to formulate and execute plans. One of us began her career as a researcher working in a large school district. In the 1970s and 80s, this meant collecting data laboriously using surveys, observations, or interviews; coding it; and entering it (via keypunched computer cards) into a massive mainframe computer for analysis. In order to do the analyses, she wrote custom computer programs. Although the work was tedious, she was one of the privileged few who had access to a computer and the skills to collect and analyze data.

In the past several decades, a great deal has changed. The twenty-first century has been dubbed the "information age." Students in school today will live their lives in the "knowledge society." There has been an exponential increase in data and information, and technology has made it available in raw and unedited forms in a range of media. Computers are commonplace, and the Internet offers unlimited access to data, undigested and often flawed.

Education, like many other fields, is awash with data. Districts and states or provinces generate huge amounts of data, and many maintain data systems that offer a wealth of potential data about schools from test results to dropout statistics, attendance figures, course enrollments, teacher credentials, student demographics, and so on.

Like many others in the society, educators are trying to come to grips with this vast deluge of new and unfiltered information and to find ways to transform data into information, then into knowledge, and ultimately into constructive action.

DATA AS A POLICY LEVER

Accountability and data are at the heart of contemporary reform efforts worldwide. Accountability has become the watchword of education, with data holding a central place in the current wave of large-scale reform. Policy makers are demanding that schools focus on achieving high standards for all students, and they are requiring evidence of progress from schools that is conceived of explicitly in a language of data (Fullan, 1999). Nations, states, provinces, and school districts have implemented large-scale assessment systems, established indicators of effectiveness, set targets, created inspection or review programs, tied rewards and sanctions to results, and many combinations of the above (Leithwood, Edge, & Jantzi, 1999; Whitty Power, & Halpin, 1998). Large-scale assessment and testing has moved from being an instrument for decision making about students to being the lever for holding schools accountable for results (Firestone, Mayrowetz, & Fairman, 1998). Leaders in states, districts, and schools are required to demonstrate their progress to the public.

As the accountability agenda has escalated, publicly reported high-profile data about schools have become a stalwart of most large-scale reform efforts (Whitty et al., 1998). In England, for example, primary school students are tested at the end of Key Stage 2 (age 11), and the percentage of pupils who meet or exceed the national target is reported for each school in the form of a league table (modeled on the mechanism for reporting the scores for soccer teams). These results are reported in national and local newspapers and are used in a myriad of ways, from decisions about support and resources available to schools to helping parents make school-choice decisions. School inspection reports are available on the Internet. Inspection reports about schools from the Office for Standards in Education (Ofstel) are posted on Web sites.

In the U.S., the No Child Left Behind (NCLB) legislation requires states, districts, and schools to report data on student achievement with measures of annual yearly progress and with analyses to show performance by gender, race, disability, income, migrant status, and English fluency. Not only are schools being judged using data, many of the reforms also assume or require a capacity on the part of schools and school leaders to use data internally to identify their priorities for change, to evaluate the impact of the decisions that they make, to understand their students' academic standing, to establish improvement plans, and to monitor and assure progress (Herman & Gribbons, 2001).

EDUCATORS' SKEPTICISM ABOUT DATA

Many school leaders find themselves caught in a "data dilemma." They mistrust data, they fear data, and many do not have the skills to use data wisely and effectively.

Mistrust of Data

There is no escaping data. Not only are school leaders surrounded by policies that require them to account using data, but they also are expected to become "data driven" themselves in their school-based planning. They are being required to use data for accountability in a politically charged environment where the stakes are high, and they are ambivalent at best and downright skeptical at worst about this shift to "data-driven" educational reform. They know that test scores and other kinds of data are used as political footballs, and data are often invoked to support narrow and parochial causes, to fight turf wars, impede change, justify a particular program, or to tie achievement to someone's leadership. Educational leaders likely *feel* or have *felt* the pressure to do well on tests and "demonstrate results."

Educators also have great confidence in the tacit knowledge that they bring to their work (i.e., personal knowledge embedded in individual experience that involves intangible factors such as personal beliefs, perspectives, and value systems). The power of educators' personal practical knowledge has long been recognized (e.g., Connelly & Clandinin, 1988) and this tacit knowledge of educational practitioners is quite resistant to change (Sykes, 1999). When exposure to data creates conditions in which educators may confront ideas and beliefs that are not consistent with their tacit knowledge or what they "believe to be true," they can challenge preconceptions that have been shaped as much out of issues of *heart* as out of issues of *head*. In all likelihood, educators' beliefs about the nature and utility of data are the result of both sets of processes. Those formed on the basis of affective responses may be resistant to change by cognitive means, while those formed on the basis of cognitive responses may be resistant to affective appeals.

Fear of Data and Evaluation

There is another interesting contributor to the way that educators feel about data and about its use for evaluative purposes. Data are really not foreign elements in schools. Educators have used data in the form of test scores, marks, and grades as the justification for evaluative judgments about students. Evaluation is pervasive in schools, but educators are the evaluators rather than the evaluated. Schools have operated on a performance orientation where success is defined in terms of recognition and high scores, and errors are unacceptable. Mistakes are to be avoided, and admission of a mistake is regarded as a weakness. Data, in this context, are punitive or rewarding but not particularly helpful.

These historical conditions conspire to create a performance-oriented, rather than a learning-oriented, culture among educators. A learning-oriented culture defines success in terms of improvement and progress and views errors as a normal part of the improvement process. Teachers and learners in a learning-oriented culture use research findings, data, and other evidence in schools as mechanisms for opening the conversation and thinking about what the errors signify, or even rethinking the issue to determine whether they are really "errors."

Lack of Training

Educators are woefully underprepared to engage in data-based decision making. Assembling good data and drawing it into a process of looking at the whole picture, understanding what the results mean, and making responsible judgments and decisions is difficult and complex.

There is little in most educators' backgrounds or training to prepare them to engage in using data or in systematic inquiry. Using data is a whole new approach to working in the culture of most schools.

For many educators, data are synonymous with statistics. The media perpetuates this belief. To complicate things, most educators likely received their introduction to basic statistical methods as a course requirement in their professional degree programs that focused on numbers and did not address the relationship of data to educational decisions. Herman and Gribbons (2001) suggest that teachers and administrators need not, indeed should not, be expected to be experts in statistics given the other obvious demands on their time—particularly teaching children. Rather, as McNamara and Thompson (n.d., p. 383) suggest, they need targeted training that:

- Places the emphasis on applications and real-world data rather than mathematical theory.
- Uses methods that allow practitioners to focus on discovery.
- Encourages a shift from calculation to interpretation.
- Makes it easier to avoid the implication that statistical analysis is strictly a matter of finding the one "right" answer.
- Provides a dynamic process for experimenting and learning from actual data.
- Uses data to uncover patterns and to generate hypotheses.
- Endorses the need to use better graphical displays and verbal statements for communication.

NEEDING TO KNOW

Schools, like many other institutions, are struggling to adapt to all of the economic, social, political, and global changes that are occurring. Communities are very diverse and mobile, so leaders are no longer intimately familiar with the community in which their school is situated. School leaders find themselves faced with the daunting task of anticipating the future and making conscious adaptations to their practices in order to keep up and to be responsive to the environment. To succeed in a rapidly changing and increasingly complex world, it is vital that schools grow, develop, adapt, and take charge of change so that they can control their own futures (Stoll, Fink & Earl, 2003). Schools that are able to take charge of change, rather than being controlled by it, are more effective and improve more rapidly than ones that are not (Gray, Hopkins, Reynolds, Wilcox, Farrell, & Jesson, 1999; Stoll & Fink, 1996; Rosenholtz, 1989).

In a world characterized by rapid change, increased complexity, and challenge, there is not enough time for adaptation by trial and error or for experimentation with fads that inevitably lose their appeal. In this context, research studies, evaluations, and routine data analyses offer mechanisms for streamlining and focusing planning and actions in schools.

Students' lives are affected profoundly by the decisions that educators make on a day-to-day basis. When policy makers and school personnel either ignore data or rely upon inadequate data, they run the risk of making poor decisions. Without good data, school personnel may be blindsided or make decisions based upon individual perceptions, opinions, and limited observations. Valuable time, energy, and resources are wasted when new programs and practices are adopted that apply foreign organizational cultures. lack evidence of effectiveness, or do not match up with student needs. The effect on students and their learning is even more important than the loss of time and energy, as another month or year passes without the implementation of effective strategies.

As Argyris and Schön (1978) argued over 20 years ago, the key challenge for any organization is not just to become more effective at performing stable tasks in the light of stable purposes but "to restructure its purposes and redefine its task in the face of a changing environment" (p. 320). Viewed from this vantage point, data are not "out there." They are, and should be, an important part of an ongoing process of analysis, insights, new learning, and changes in practice in all schools and districts. Data provide tools for the investigation necessary to plan appropriate and focused improvement strategies. Synthesizing and organizing data in different ways stimulates reflection and conjecture about the nature of the problem under consideration. Over time, this process gives rise to defensible plans for changes. Thus, while the effective use of data may be time-consuming and difficult initially, it is well worth the effort in the long run. School personnel who understand their students' needs and use data about their school communities in the service of those needs are better prepared to make informed decisions, remain better focused throughout implementation, recognize whether their efforts are effective, and are more capable of institutionalizing change and improving continuously (Education Commission of the States, 2000).

If data are to become part of the fabric of school improvement, leaders in schools and districts must become active players in the data-rich environment that surrounds them so that they have more and better information available on which to base decisions (Earl, 1998). They need to incorporate a "system of use" for interpreting and acting on information into schools and districts (Earl & LeMahieu, 1997). Like everything else that is bombarding leaders, becoming a skilled and confident consumer and user of data is not simple or straightforward. It requires acquiring a new range of leadership capacities. But using data is not a mechanistic process. It is a skill and an art and a way of thinking that includes an understanding of the nature of evidence, from its definition and collection to its interpretation and presentation (Katz, Sutherland & Earl, 2002).

THINKING DIFFERENTLY ABOUT DATA

The "theory of action" underlying large-scale reform policy agenda like No Child Left Behind (U.S.) and Every Child Matters (U.K.) is that once schools have the necessary data, educators will be in a position to diagnose areas of strength and areas in need of improvement. They will then adjust structures and practices in ways that will impact positively on student learning and this, in turn, will lead to enhanced student achievement for all students. Thus, the capacity requirement underlying such policies is that educators know how to use data in order to make the necessary consequent decisions.

The important distinction to make is between the "theory of action" as intent and the foundational capacities on which it rests. We believe that the large-scale accountability climate has the potential to set the necessary theory of action in place. Few would argue with the inherent logic of data-driven decision making. Moreover, the advent of high-profile accountability policies has likely functioned as an extrinsic motivator, encouraging engagement with an agenda (in this case data-driven decision making) that might otherwise remain in the background. But this alone is not enough. Katz, Sutherland, and Earl (2002) point out that the challenge is to follow this engagement with intentional opportunities to develop intrinsic practices in order to build the necessary capacities in such a way that they become habitual aspects of school work and do not remain at the mercy of a policy-bound extrinsic benefactor. For many, this approach will require thinking differently about using data. Subscription to the theory of action is necessary but not enough. Without new learning that is deliberate and disciplined, the possibility for subversion of intent is very real. Data, rather than being understood as information for an accountability system, can be seen as the accountability system itself. Unintended consequences of the sort that have been well documented by Linda Darling-Hammond (2004) can follow—teacher morale can fade, the most vulnerable students may be sidelined, and the curriculum can narrow, to name just a few examples.

All of their past experiences form the basis for educators' beliefs about using data. Their views are a product of their ways of thinking and of what they have come to know. Human beings are all predisposed to preserve existing understandings of the world. We all attempt to make new things familiar by transforming them to be consistent with what we already know (or believe to be true). If people did not do this, they would be overwhelmed by the sheer volume of novelty that would emerge around every corner. But such preservation and conservation make it difficult for people to engage in what psychologists call conceptual change—*real* changes in how and what they think and know that enable them to see the world differently.

We believe that learning to use data for school improvement in the way that is described in this book is a conceptual change. The National Research Council's synthesized report on how people learn (Donovan, Bransford & Pellegrino, 2000) spells out three overarching cognitive themes that rest on a solid research base and that can be taken to explicate the process of conceptual change referenced above. Paraphrased for brevity and translated into the language of data-driven decision making by Katz, Sutherland and Earl (in press), they are:

- Individuals hold preconceptions about the nature and utility of data. If these initial understandings are not engaged, they may fail to grasp the new concepts and information to which they are exposed, or they may learn them solely for the purposes of an external mandate and then revert to their preconceptions once it is removed.
- To develop competence in the processes and practices surrounding the use of data for wise decision making, individuals must have a foundation of declarative and procedural knowledge and understand these ideas in the context of a conceptual framework that facilitates application.
- "Metacognitive" or reflective opportunities can help individuals take control over their own learning by defining goals and monitoring the progress towards their achievement.

We have tried to honor these cognitive themes in the remainder of this book by developing a process that makes preconceptions explicit, creating assignments, giving ideas about further reading to help educators develop a knowledge base, and providing opportunities for reflection.

October 26—Janet, the principal of H. C. Andersen Middle School, is sitting at her desk looking worried. A mountain of paper sits in front of her. She just stares. What is she going to do? She rereads the memo from her superintendent:

Once again, as part of our accountability and improvement strategy, each school in the district will use the attached electronic template to produce an improvement plan for the school. The improvement plan should detail the school's accomplishments, difficulties, action plans, and targets. These plans should be evidence-based, drawing on systemwide and local data. The completed document should be sent to the superintendent's office for review no later than January 20. The plans will form the basis for each school's annual review and will be included in a district report that will be published in the spring for public distribution.

Janet is troubled. She realizes that it is important to plan for improvement and share what the school is doing with the community.

She agrees that schools need to be accountable and that they should be more systematic in their planning and in how they organize their improvement program. Janet also knows that an improvement plan for the school would be part of her job as principal. She was part of the process at her last school. It isn't that she doesn't want to do it. But she isn't sure that completing this template will really change anything in the school. She is also worried because district administrators will be using this report as the basis for their appraisal of the school, maybe even to decide about resource allocation—not to mention that she is expected to put the report on the school's Web site and to use it as an information bulletin for parents. And they want it to be evidence-based, whatever that means. Presumably that means using data, but what data should she use? The template has a space for the results from the district and state tests, but there is loads of room for the school to add "local data." Well, she knows that they surveyed the parents before they decided about the new playground equipment, and she could probably get some statistics about something or other from the district office. But that won't tell much about H. C. Andersen. Somehow, it just doesn't feel right.

School leaders everywhere are struggling with the same issues as Janet. They are required to prepare reports about their schools for public distribution and need to decide what to do. At the same time, they all operate in different policy contexts, depending on the country, state, or province and district in which they are located.

ACCOUNTABILITY REDEFINED

When all is said and done, school leaders are the ones who are accountable for the work of the school, and most of the leaders that we know are happy and willing to have this responsibility. At the same time, they are not always sure what "being accountable" means. Sometimes they feel like helpless victims, responding to requirements from outside that do not really fit with what they see in their schools. At the same time, they are exhorted to be responsive to their local communities and to ensure that they are serving their students well. In theory, accountability sounds wonderful. In practice, it raises a host of thorny issues, not the least of which is a philosophical one—What does accountability mean? There is no blueprint that defines accountability, and a number of very different understandings prevail.

Linda Darling-Hammond (1994) describes two different views of educational change and of accountability:

> One view seeks to induce change through extrinsic rewards and sanctions both schools and students, on the assumption that the fundamental problem is a lack of will to change on the part of educators. The other view seeks to induce change by building knowledge among school practitioners and parents about alternative methods and by stimulating organizational rethinking through opportunities to work together on the design of teaching and schooling and to experiment with new approaches. This view assumes that the fundamental problem is a lack of knowledge about the possibilities for teaching and learning, combined with lack of organizational capacity for change. (p. 23)

Policy makers often try to appeal to both camps by embracing common standards and individual variation, numerical comparability and descriptive sensitivity, assessment designed to improve student learning, and assessment that placates demands for systemwide accountability (Hargreaves, Earl & Schmidt, 2002).

> **Accounting** is gathering, organizing, and reporting information that describes performance
>
> **Accountability** is the conversation about what the information means and how it fits with everything else that we know and about how to use it to make positive changes.
> —Earl and LeMahieu, 1997

The premise underlying this book is that the dichotomy will persist and that educational accountability will always be a mixture of the two views and each of them has a role to play in how change happens.

High-stakes accountability systems can create a sense of urgency and provide "pressure" for change. However, real accountability is much more than *accounting* (providing information or justifications in an annual report or a press release or even student report cards). It is a moral and professional responsibility to be knowledgeable and fair in teaching and in interactions with students and their parents. It engenders respect, trust, shared understanding, and mutual support.

CHOOSING ACCOUNTABILITY THROUGH INFORMED PROFESSIONAL JUDGMENT

Michael Barber (2001), a national policy advisor on education in England, uses the following graphic to describe trends in educational reform over the past 50 years as a function of the knowledge base on which it has been founded and the locus of responsibility and decision making.

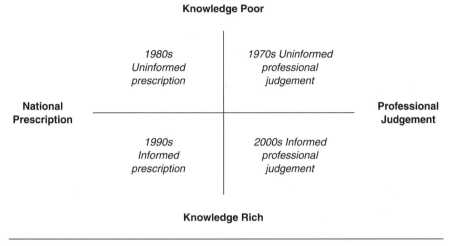

Knowledge Poor

1980s Uninformed prescription	1970s Uninformed professional judgement

National Prescription — **Professional Judgement**

1990s Informed prescription	2000s Informed professional judgement

Knowledge Rich

SOURCE: Barber, 2001

He portrays the 1970s as a time of "uninformed professional judgment" in which educators operated largely as individuals within broad policy guidelines and relied on their personal professional perspectives to make decisions. This was the era of "leave us alone to teach." The 1980s were a time of "uninformed prescription" where governments took direct control of education and dictated prescriptive directions, often without appealing to any knowledge base other than their own ideological views. National or federal programs proliferated, with centrally directed curriculum and assessment systems. In the 1990s governments still controlled the educational agenda, but they began to draw on research and other evidence to inform their policies.

Barber sees the 2000s as an era of "informed professional judgment" in which control of education ought to be returned to educators, but now with explicit requirements to be informed professionals. And that means using evidence and research to justify and support educational decisions.

We believe that school leaders who are frustrated with the prescriptive policies of the past few decades and with accountability systems that "name, shame, and blame" schools are ready to take control of the accountability agenda. They are ready for "informed professionalism," but that requires a concerted emphasis on becoming and staying "informed."

> Give us the accounting and we'll do the accountability.
> —Workshop participant (Principal)

> Accountability without improvement is empty rhetoric.
>
> Improvement without accountability is whimsical action without direction.
>
> —Earl, quoted in Education Quality and Accountability Office (EQAO), 2002

School leaders find themselves faced with messy situations that have more than a single right answer and demand reflective judgments. They are faced with the daunting task of anticipating the future and making conscious adaptations to their practices in order to keep up and to be responsive to an ever-changing environment. We believe that the essence of accountability is a deep and abiding commitment to making schools as good as they can be for all students.

Janet wants to be accountable, but she isn't at all sure that completing the district template and posting it on the school Web site will give her the kind of accountability that she wants. The more that she thinks about H. C. Andersen, the more she believes that there is lots of room for improvement and that she needs to foster a system of internal accountability where the staff as a whole is interested in making changes that will actually improve learning for the kids.

Moving to informed professional judgment is paradoxical, by definition. On one hand, it puts educational reform squarely in the hands of educational professionals. At the same time, it means that educators cannot rely on tacit knowledge and personal preferences. Instead, they must be prepared to challenge and reconstruct their professional knowledge and to change their practice (Hannay, Mahony & MacFarlane, 2004). This shift means that educators need to get comfortable with using data and evidence as tools in routine critical inquiry about what they do.

THE ROLE OF DATA IN INFORMED PROFESSIONAL JUDGMENT

Educators are recognizing that they need to use data even though they do not always do it very well. They are aware that we live in a knowledge society in which having and using knowledge wisely is an essential skill. It makes sense that leaders will make better decisions when they use information to help clarify issues, identify alternative solutions to problems, and target resources more effectively. There is not enough time for adaptation by trial and error or for experimentation with fads that inevitably lose their appeal.

Professional accountability is based on data, not as a final judgment but as part of the toolkit for understanding current performance and formulating plans for reasonable actions (Earl & LeMahieu, 1997). Educational leaders and school staffs who are committed to professional accountability and making informed professional judgments think of accountability not as a static numerical accounting but as a conversation, using data to stimulate discussion, challenge ideas, rethink directions, and monitor progress, providing an ongoing image of their school as it changes, progresses, stalls, regroups, and moves forward again.

This makes accountability emotional, personal, and political, reflecting all of the points of view that exist within the school community. Instead of being a point of contention, data can provide the vehicle for moving the community forward in ways that strengthen the bonds of shared vision and forge the relationships needed to serve that vision. Accountability and data are right in the center of the conversation, not as instruments of naming and blaming but as the grist for discussing policies and practices in conversations that nourish the collective will for action. Educators themselves become the prime consumers of data as they work towards making reasoned decisions about their actions in the school and sharing their thinking and their work with parents, students, and others in the community who care about education.

As the following table from the Education Commission of the States shows, data can be used for many different and important decisions.

	Common Uses of Data
Discover Issues	Reveal issues and problems that may otherwise remain hidden. Ascertain the needs of students, educators, parents, and other community members. Ensure that no students fall through the cracks. Identify grade-level and schoolwide strengths and weaknesses.
Diagnose Situations	Understand the root causes of problems. Comprehend why some students are not performing well. Determine eligibility for special programs. Target specific areas for improvement. Provide criteria for focusing on high priority goals.
Forecast Future Conditions	Predict the needs of future students, educators, parents, and community members. Suggest possible local, regional, state, or national trends that will affect the school and the programs offered. Surmise types of programs required. Infer types of expertise needed.
Improve Policy and Practice	Reform teaching and learning. Enhance instruction and assessment. Guide curriculum development, revision, and alignment.

(Continued)

	Common Uses of Data
	Build a culture of inquiry and continuous improvement.
	Guide the allocation of resources.
	Avoid quick fixes and one-size-fits-all solutions.
Evaluate Effectiveness	Understand and describe high-quality performance.
	Provide feedback to students, teachers, and administrators about their performance.
	Measure program effectiveness.
	Identify practices that produce desired results.
	Convince stakeholders of the need for change.
	Highlight successes.
Promote Accountability	Monitor and document progress toward achieving goals.
	Inform internal and external stakeholders of progress.
	Confirm or discredit assumptions about students and school practices.
	Develop meaningful responses to criticism.
	Meet state and federal reporting requirements.
	Ensure that all personnel are focused on student learning.

SOURCE: Education Commission of the States, 2000

When educators consider lots of data, both positive and negative, they are more likely to reach a decision that everyone can live with because everyone has access to the same information. Nothing is withheld, and everyone has to stop and think about how their ideas fit with the data.

USING DATA TO "TAKE CHARGE OF CHANGE"

Schools that are able to use data to take charge of change are more effective and improve more rapidly than ones that are not (Gray et al., 1999; Rosenholtz, 1989; Stoll & Fink, 1996). But using data is something that makes many educators feel uncomfortable. The school reform movement is calling for proof—tangible, valid evidence that what schools are doing is working, that students are learning faster and better.

Using data does not have to be a mechanical or technical process that denigrates educators' intuition, teaching philosophy, and personal experience. In fact, using data wisely is a human thinking activity that draws on personal views but also on capturing and organizing ideas in some systematic way, turning the information into meaningful actions and making the interpretation public and transparent (Senge, 1990). Having data is a beginning, but it is not enough. Schools need to move from being data-rich to being information-rich and knowledge-rich as well.

Viewed from this vantage point, using data is not separate from planning and from routine decisions in schools. Instead, data are a necessary part of an ongoing process of analysis, insight, new learning, and changes in practice. Synthesizing and organizing data in different ways stimulates reflection and conjecture about the nature of the problem under consideration and provides the vehicle for investigating and planning focused improvement strategies.

Information becomes knowledge when it is shaped, organized, and embedded in a context that gives it meaning and connectedness. The implications for leaders are vast. In the next chapter we outline some of the capacities that educational leaders will need to develop to lead in a data-rich world.

Janet, sitting quietly at her desk, is resolved. The more she has thought about it, the more she is determined that the process is going to serve some real benefit for H. C. Andersen. There is lots of work to do. Why not make it a data-driven (or at least a data-informed) process that moves the whole school forward?

Assignment #2

Your Policy Context

Think about your local policy context and history and use Task Sheet #2 in the Resource section to describe what accountability currently means to you, the expectations for accountability in your school (by national, state or province, or district policy makers), and reflect on your current accountability practices. After you have considered your current practices, think about what accountability could mean to you and how it could be different.

Using Data for Informed Decision Making

Making a move from accountability as surveillance to accountability for improvement situates educators as the prime consumers of data in order to make informed decisions. This means thinking about accountability and using data as a part of a leader's repertoire for organizational improvement, not because it is mandated but because data can provide a window into the workings of the school that contribute to routinely rethinking and reconstructing professional knowledge and changing practices.

Becoming a skilled and confident consumer and user of data is not simple or straightforward; nor is it a mechanistic process. It is a skill and an art and a way of thinking that includes an understanding of the nature of evidence, from its definition and collection to its interpretation and presentation (Katz, Sutherland & Earl, 2002). In another publication we have identified what we believe are the key capacities for leaders in a data-rich world (Earl & Katz, 2002). For informed professionalism, leaders will need to:

- develop an inquiry habit of mind,
- become data literate, and
- create a culture of inquiry in their school community.

In this chapter, we give a general description of each of these capacities. In Chapters 4, 5, and 6 we revisit each of them in more detail, with examples from H. C. Andersen Middle School and tasks to give the readers practice in developing their own capacities.

AN INQUIRY HABIT OF MIND

Leaders who use data productively have a mind set of being in charge of their own destiny, always needing to know more, and creating or locating the knowledge that will be useful to them along the way. As Senge (cited in Stoll, Fink, & Earl, 2003, p. 132) said, a learning organization is one that is "continually expanding its capacity to create its future." It is not a linear or mechanistic process but an iterative process of "thinking in circles" (O'Connor & McDermott, 1997) with a series of decisions, actions, and feedback loops guiding the process. In this kind of school, leaders are not technicians organizing and manipulating data in prescribed ways, like following a paint-by-number picture; they develop an "inquiry habit of mind," collecting and interpreting evidence in ways that advance their understanding. Habits of mind incorporate dispositional, emotional, motivational, and personality variables that contribute to competence in managing the environment and making decisions (Keating, 1996). We link *inquiry* to *habit of mind* to emphasize a way of thinking that is a dynamic iterative system to organize ideas, seek out information, and move closer and closer to understanding some phenomenon. What does this mean for school leaders? A school leader with *an inquiry habit of mind:*

- *Values Deep Understanding.* Leaders with an inquiry habit of mind do not presume an outcome; instead they allow for a range of outcomes and keep searching for increased understanding and clarity.
- *Reserves Judgment and Has a Tolerance for Ambiguity.* Learning from data requires a tolerance for uncertainty and a willingness to live in the dissonance long enough to investigate and explore ideas until there is some clarity about what it might mean.
- *Takes a Range of Perspectives and Systematically Poses Increasingly Focused Questions.* Data almost never provide answers. Instead, using data usually leads to more and more focused investigation and to better questions.

DATA LITERACY

There is probably nothing in education that garners more public attention than data about schools. However, interpretation and application of data by educators, and by the public, are often woefully inadequate and sometimes very wrong. If school leaders are going to be active in interpreting and using data, as well as in challenging and disputing interpretations or uses that they believe are contestable, they must become "data-literate." A *data-literate* leader:

- *Thinks About Purpose(s).* No doctor would take a patient's temperature and use it to ascertain their cardiovascular fitness; neither would pilots be content with wind speed as the only data needed to plan transatlantic flights. All too often, educational decisions get made using no data or available data rather than appropriate data. Data-literate leaders realize that they need different data for different purposes.

- *Recognizes Sound and Unsound Data.* Data are numbers or words or pictures that represent some underlying ideas. They are estimates, with some degree of uncertainty, not absolute measurements. One of the first challenges for anyone interpreting data is to ascertain the quality of the data that they intend to use. Bad data can contribute to bad decisions. For some leaders, the existence of flawed data is sufficient reason to ignore or mistrust data altogether. But to blame the data is unreasonable. When people use words to make false claims or offer unreasonable ideas, we don't blame the English language. Rather than trashing all statements with numbers in them, a more reasonable response is to learn enough about the statistics to distinguish honest, useful conclusions from skullduggery or foolishness (Abelson, 1995).

- *Is Knowledgeable About Statistical and Measurement Concepts.* Data in education are generally measurements or records of something, often analyzed using statistics. But statistics strike fear into the hearts of many people. For the most part, educators have not seen statistics as a useful addition to their tool kit for decision making. Instead, statistics are either imbued with a magical quality of numerical "truth," or they are mistrusted as blatant attempts to distort or to manipulate an audience. Neither of these positions is defensible. Tests and statistical procedures have been developed to try to provide *estimates* of invisible human qualities such as achievement or creativity. And there are conventions and rules for the measurement of student achievement that are extremely important, especially when the results are being used to make significant decisions. If leaders are going to use data to enhance rather than distort educational decisions, they have a responsibility to understand the principles that underlie the statistics.

- *Recognizes Other Kinds of Data.* Although we often equate data with numbers, statistics are not the only kinds of data that leaders can utilize. Opinions, anecdotes, and observations are all acceptable as data. There are some criteria, however, that need to be met for something to qualify as data. It is not enough to troll about looking for perspectives that support an existing system of beliefs. Genuine inquiry requires that qualitative data also be collected in some systematic way and organized and analyzed to allow various views to be expressed and incorporated into the interpretation.

- *Makes Interpretation Paramount.* Data and statistics may provide the tools for measuring educational concepts, but the numbers are only as good as the thinking and interpretation. Data do not provide right answers or quick fixes. Instead, they are necessary but not sufficient elements of the conversations that ensue. Data offer decision makers an opportunity to view a phenomenon through a number of different lenses, to put forward hypotheses, to challenge beliefs, and to pose more questions. Interpretation requires time, thoughtfulness, reservation of judgments, and open challenge of, as well as support for, ideas. Interpretation, then, is thinking—formulating possibilities, developing convincing arguments, locating logical flaws, and establishing a feasible and defensible notion of what the data represent. In the hands of effective leaders, data become information, and the information is transformed into knowledge and even wisdom.

- *Pays Attention to Reporting and to Audiences.* Not only do data provide lenses for seeing more clearly, leaders can use data to explain and justify their decisions to those who care to know. Jaeger and others (1993) found that reports prepared for parents about schools did not contain the information parents considered most important for them. They were also misinterpreted by 30–50% of the parents who received them. Attention to audience, presentation of data, interpretation, and key messages cannot be overlooked as essential elements in using data wisely.

A CULTURE OF INQUIRY

School leaders have little chance of using data unless the school as a whole is also committed to being a community, routinely challenging existing beliefs and practices, and using data to make sense of their environment and to think about their future. This means a dramatic shift in mind set for the whole school so that data become a core part of school culture, even a topic of staff room conversation and classroom practice. Leaders have the challenge of convincing everyone who works in the school of the merits of using data for productive change and creating the conditions in which data can become an integral part of school decision making. In order to create a *culture of inquiry,* a leader:

- *Involves Others in Interpreting and Engaging With the Data.* New insights do not happen by osmosis. They come from facing ideas that challenge the familiar ways of viewing issues. They happen in the dissonance and in the construction of new and shared meaning. Leaders contribute to a culture of inquiry by providing opportunities for others to become inquiry-minded and data literate. This means facilitating, sponsoring, mentoring, and convincing others to engage with the data and think about it, even (and especially) when it is hard work. Fullan (1999) describes learning communities as places where "interaction inside and outside the organization converts tacit knowledge to explicit knowledge on an ongoing basis" (p.16). But, all too often, "new insights fail to get put into practice because they conflict with deeply held internal images of how the world works" (Senge, 1990, p. 174). Data can offer a vehicle for investigating tacit knowledge to refine and even transform it as it is converted into explicit knowledge for use in making institutional decisions.

- *Stimulates an Internal Sense of "Urgency."* Data can be a powerful mechanism for refocusing the agenda or recasting the problem. No school is as good as it can be; there are always areas that deserve attention. Data become the window for identifying "what next" and instilling "urgency" as a way of unleashing the energy associated with embarking on a course of action that makes sense in fulfilling the moral purpose of schooling (Earl & Lee, 1998).

- *Makes Time.* Making sense of data and using it to come to collective meaning and commitment is not an overnight process, and it does not happen in one shot. Leaders and the people who work with them are going to need time, and lots of it—to think about the important issues, to decide what data are relevant and make sure they have it, to consider the data and try to make sense of it, to argue and challenge and reflect, to get more information, to argue and challenge and reflect again, to formulate and reformulate action plans, to prepare thoughtful and accessible ways to share their learning with the community, and to stand back to consolidate what they have learned. Luckily the time spent will be an investment in organizational learning and better decision making, but leaders have the task of managing this precious commodity to ensure that important things are done well.

- *Uses "Critical Friends."* The idea of *critical friends* is a powerful one. Friends bring a high degree of positive regard, are forgiving, and are tolerant of failings. Critics are often conditional, negative, and intolerant of failure. Critical friends offer both support and critique in an open, honest appraisal (MacBeath, 1998). As Costa and Kallick (1995) describe it, a critical friend is "a trusted person who asks provocative questions, provides data to be examined through another lens, and offers critique of a person's work, as a friend" (p. 154). External critical friends with expertise in data collection, interpretation, and use, as well as sensitivity and the ability to listen and think on their feet, come without vested interests and can build trust and bring a dispassionate perspective. They can observe what may not be apparent to insiders, facilitate reflection on the issues that arise, explain complex data in accessible ways, ask questions, probe for justification and evidence to support perceptions, and help reformulate interpretations. They are not afraid to challenge assumptions, beliefs, or simplistic interpretations in a nonjudgmental and helpful way. Critical friends are well-placed to remind the participants of what they have accomplished and facilitate their movement towards the next goals.

LEADING IN A DATA-RICH WORLD

Although data have become central to educational decision making, most educators do not have a comfort level with data interpretation or use and often experience data anxiety. Most do not have the background, skills, or dispositions described above.

Janet is well aware that she is a little spooked by the idea of using data. The last time she studied anything statistical was in beginning psychology, and she had completely forgotten most of it. Anyway, it didn't really seem as if the material that she has studied was very relevant to using data in a real school setting. She wanted to learn more but she was really not sure where to go or what she needed to know. And she wanted it to be useful, not just abstract theories.

Assignment #3

Capacities for Leading in a Data-Rich World

You may feel the same as Janet did. So, it is time to reflect on your own capacities in relation to the capacities outlined in this chapter. Use Task Sheet #3 in the Resource section to do a self-assessment of your personal situation in relation to inquiry habit of mind, data literacy, and a culture of inquiry in your school community.

Cultivating the Qualities of Data-Driven Leadership

As we see it, school leaders can take charge of change and use data as a powerful tool for making wise and timely decisions that are consistent with the exigencies of their local contexts and responsive to their unique perspectives, not by slavishly applying external standards to their work or by plotting to ensure that they meet their targets. Rather, they can create their own future through careful planning, honest appraisal, and professional learning always focused on improved conditions for teaching and learning as a way of being.

In this chapter we offer a metaphor for using data for improvement in which school leaders (formal and informal) are likened to artists. Artists are always driven by data—by the colors, textures, and images that they observe, investigate, and respond to. They use their talent to decide what to emphasize and how to communicate a mood and a message to the audience. This metaphor of school leaders as artists offers an alternate view to an image of leaders as automatons, using data to paint by numbers on a canvas designed by someone far away. Leadership teams are producers of images of their schools and of their educational futures.

THE PAINTING METAPHOR

Collecting and using data in schools is like painting a series of pictures—pictures that are subtle and changeable and capture the nuances of the subject. This is a far cry from stick drawing or paint by numbers. Imagine the experiences of Monet as he wandered through his beautiful garden at Giverny at different times of the day and the year from different directions, paying attention to different colors or textures or designs. His work was always driven by data—by the colors, shadows, textures, and images that he observed, investigated, and responded to. He immersed himself in the place that was Giverny and used his considerable interpretative skill to draw the salient features to the foreground, emphasize important dimensions, and share his experiences with his audience. And he did not paint one picture and call it Giverny. He painted hundreds, each capturing some of the subtleties of the world he inhabited. His work inspired others to think about the world in which they live and even to rethink the art of painting itself. Although Monet no longer paints his beautiful garden, Giverny is now a public park, and artists from all over the world travel to see it and to create their own representations of this famous landscape—some of them continuing the impressionist style, others using very different approaches.

Like Monet, leaders can be producers of images of their schools and of their educational futures. Data are the colors available to them to investigate and represent their world. And data, like colors on a palette, need a talented artist to bring them to life. Just as the paint tubes provide a mechanism for portraying the flowers in the garden, data describe ideas or concepts but need wisdom and experience to give them meaning.

We believe that educators should think about the important planning and improvement decisions that they have to make and systematically use data to make informed professional judgments in the same way that an artist thinks about creating a gallery full of paintings. Educators, like artists, engage in a continuous process of thinking and rethinking what needs to be done, how well the choices are working, what comes next, and how their work needs to be communicated to and shared with others. Data provide the "stuff" to think about, the evidence that can confirm or challenge what educators "believe to be true," and the stimulus for conversations among themselves and with others about "making this school better and better."

In the remainder of this book, we use this metaphor of educators as painters working together to capture the myriad and changeable images that matter about their school and presenting these images to a range of audiences as the basis for their ongoing decision making. Sometimes the paintings will be completed individually, as teachers or leaders work on their own. In other cases, educators will work in teams to create a collage or a mural of their thinking and their work. In all cases, they are drawing on many sources of information to construct a coherent and distinctive image of where they are now, where they want to be in the future, and how they might go about bridging the gap. Finally, educators will paint many pictures, not just one, with different purposes, audiences, and issues to consider.

Most painters, even those who appear to be undisciplined and random in their actions, go through a great deal of thinking and planning before they ever begin to paint. Once they have a notion of the content, mood, and image that they hope to capture, they rely on having well-developed technical skills to select their palette and execute the process of painting, all the while making adjustments, changing ideas, and rethinking their vision. Educational teams can follow the same principles when they appeal to data in their improvement process. All too often, educators jump to the data prematurely and get lost in the details. They attend to the data that they have rather than thinking about the data that they need. Instead, our model begins with thinking and planning, with data as a tool along the way. The following figure shows the process of using data to paint pictures of school improvement, using the capacities for leaders—inquiry habit of mind, data literacy, and a culture of inquiry—as a primary organizer for the stages in painting.

Painting as a Metaphor for Making Data-Informed Decisions					
Inquiry Habit of Mind		**Data Literacy**		**Culture of Inquiry**	
Setting the Canvas	**Planning This Picture**	**Blocking the Canvas**	**The First Strokes**	**The Image Grows**	**Displaying the Picture**
What is our purpose? What roles do we play? Who are the audiences?	What do we *think* we know? Where do we want to go?	What do we want (or need) to know? What data do we need? How good are these data?	How do we make sense of this? What does it all mean?	What does this picture include? What will we do as a result of our new knowledge?	How will we engage the audience? How will we share what we have learned?

Educators need to use data in many different contexts—to establish their current state, to determine improvement plans, to chart effectiveness of their initiatives, and to monitor their progress towards their goals. This process can serve a model at any stage in their planning and as a guide as they become comfortable with using data in their work. The process is organized around the three major capacities required by leaders in a data-rich world from the prior chapter. The panels in the graphic use the painting metaphor to detail the process of using data.

INQUIRY HABIT OF MIND

The first stage of the process is both simple and profound. Professional decisions in schools have historically been based on tacit knowledge, knowledge that is embedded in individual experiences and involves intangible factors like personal belief and values. For the most part, educators continue to do what they have always done, and they do it pretty well. These self-selected and self-directed choices are often conservative and resistant to fundamental change (Sykes, 1999; Putnam & Borko, 1997). But schools today are very complex places, and the kinds of challenges that school leaders face are often ill-structured, with more than a single right answer. Such problems demand reflection, consideration of many points of view, and attention to context and evidence. As Fullan (2001) argues:

> Schools are beginning to discover that new ideas, knowledge creation, inquiry and sharing are essential to solving learning problems in a rapidly changing society. (p. xi)

We believe the term *inquiry habit of mind* is particularly appropriate to describe this process-oriented mode of thought that organizational leaders must develop in the service of making wise decisions. Costa and Kallick (2000) define "habits of mind" as broad, enduing learnings that require a discipline of the mind that is practiced so that it becomes a habitual way of working toward more thoughtful, intelligent action. So, an *inquiry habit of mind* for organizational improvement means developing a habit of using inquiry and reflection to think about where you are, where you are going, how you will get there, and then rethinking the whole process to see how well it is working and making adjustments.

Setting the Canvas

Setting the Canvas

Why is this issue an important area to pay attention to?

What is prompting this decision?

Who will be influenced by it?

Who needs to be involved?

What is our role in this decision?

Artists begin their work by preparing their canvas and deciding about the dimensions and scope of the work. For educational leaders, setting the canvas means establishing the background for an issue, deciding why they are dedicating resources (especially time) to this issue, and identifying all of the people who need to be involved in one way or another. Before making any serious educational decisions, the leadership team needs to be explicit about their purpose and who should be involved in the decision, about the audience for the judgment, and about their own responsibility in the decision making process.

Planning This Picture

In the second stage, the team situates the issue by establishing the current state of affairs and explicitly deciding about the ideal outcome of their work. It is important to have a clear picture of the present before jumping into making plans and some image of what you are hoping to accomplish.

> **Planning This Picture**
>
> Where are we now?
>
> What do we think we know?
>
> Where do we want to go?

DATA LITERACY

Most school districts have lots of data available in their district information systems, although they may not be easily accessible or organized in a way that can be easily used by individual schools. Schools are also likely to have various kinds of other formal and informal data that tend not to be electronically stored—data like classroom records, classroom assessments, and program descriptions. Educators can draw on many different forms of evidence—research studies, test results, surveys, observations, testimonies, and witnesses all qualify as data. The challenges come in deciding what data are appropriate and useful for their purposes, ensuring the quality of the data, and doing the kinds of analyses and interpretations that will help them make sense of the data.

Blocking the Canvas

Once the team has a beginning feel of the contours of the issue, they can begin to think about what data will help them make the image visible to themselves and others. They are ready to decide what data they need—to choose their palette of colors, define the scope of the work, and make decisions about composition and design. This is not as simple a process as it may appear. Getting the right data depends on asking the right questions.

> **Blocking the Canvas**
>
> What are we trying to understand better?
>
> What is the focus of this picture?
>
> What do we need to know to capture the complexity?
>
> What data do we need?

The First Strokes

The value associated with data come from skill in discerning the quality of the data, organizing it, thinking about what it might mean, and using it wisely to make decisions. Making sense of data, like painting pictures, is an iterative process. One idea leads to another. Some ideas lose credibility in the process. Others get clearer. New information leads the work in a different direction.

The First Strokes

How do we make sense of these data?

What help do we need to analyze and interpret the data?

How much confidence do we have in these data?

What are the limitations of the data?

What can we learn from the data?

What other data do we need?

In this stage, the team considers data in a range of different configurations; spends time trying to make sense of it through analysis, discussion, and interpretation; and transforms data into knowledge that they can use. This is the process that determines what the picture looks like—what story it tells, what images come into foreground and what ones recede into background, what mood it creates, etc.

This is where technical assistance becomes an important part of the process. Educators are not likely to have the technical expertise to do all of the necessary analyses, and they do not need to become data analysts. What is much more important is that leaders are aware of the values and the constraints that are associated with various kinds of data as they use it to think about their work. Then they can call on others to serve as "critical friends" to help them with analysis and even with the interpretation.

A CULTURE OF INQUIRY

This book is premised on a belief that educational change depends on collaborative professional learning. We have known for a long time that mandating change does not work. Mandates may create an awareness that changes are necessary, but real change depends on people working in schools engaging in new learning, individually and collectively, to refresh their knowledge, understandings, and skills and to deal with and take charge of change.

There is a good deal of research to support a conviction that professional learning communities can generate and support sustainable improvements because they build the necessary professional skill and capacity to keep schools progressing. Hord (1997) describes a professional community of learners as one in which the teachers and administrators continuously seek and share learning and act on their learning. The goal of their actions is to enhance their effectiveness as professionals for the students' benefit; thus, this arrangement may also be termed *communities of continuous inquiry and improvement.*

In our view, becoming inquiry-minded and data literate are major changes in practice that are consistent with the notion of professional learning communities and that warrant concerted attention to new shared learning. When educators come to the planning process as investigators, wanting to understand and interested in working together and with others to find the best solutions, they find themselves engaged in a very different kind of organization that values dissenting voices and is determined to generate and share knowledge, even when the new knowledge may mean having to make dramatic changes and even reinvent itself.

The Image Grows

As the team considers the data and talks about what they are learning, their painting begins to materialize, and they become more aware that there are many possible interpretations and many possible strategies for improving what they do in schools. But even more important, the data suggest that there is work to be done. It is time to use their new learning to change what they are doing.

Displaying the Picture

The team also finds that they are not alone. There are many people in the community who care deeply about what happens in schools. They can start to think about what they need to communicate to whom and about how others can contribute to their ongoing quest for deeper understanding and better solutions.

> **Displaying the Picture**
>
> How will we engage the audience?
>
> How will we share what we have learned?

The painting metaphor gives the leadership team a process for using data to produce a static image of an issue at a point in time. Once there is an initial image, it becomes the basis for public engagement and for changing practices.

In this metaphor, the picture is the stimulus for action, not the end result. The process now shifts to sharing what has been learned, listening carefully to the responses from the various people who care, and deciding what has to happen next. This is not a showcase event; it is an ongoing, active exchange of ideas and decisions about action.

A GALLERY FULL OF PAINTINGS

Using data to make decisions is hard work. Although it may be tempting to mount the picture and accept the accolades, educational change is a never-ending process, and there is never a single final image. Instead, each image is one in a series that will emerge as the team revisits the issue and considers what has changed and what needs adjustment. When schools engage in ongoing school improvement, they find themselves in a continuous cycle of change. It gets easier as they internalize and embed the technical skills, organizational processes, and values into routines in the culture of the school.

> **A Gallery Full of Paintings**
>
> How are we doing?
>
> What other issues do we need to address?
>
> How do we keep the appeal to data as a routine part of our planning and improvement process?

In the following chapters, Janet and her team at H. C. Andersen Middle School are engaged in an initial process of using data to see where they are and where they are going. As time goes on, they will use the same process to track their progress and to revisit their focus. They will have many different data pictures to show their development and decision making, and the collection will form an historical and conceptual account of their journey, of their progress, and of their learning.

Developing an Inquiry Habit of Mind

This chapter describes a process for developing an inquiry habit of mind by going through the first stages of preparing to paint—setting the canvas and planning this picture.

SETTING THE CANVAS

This is the first stage of your process—getting comfortable with the idea of intentionally planning your work and being prepared to make changes, sometimes radical and sometimes not, to the way you do business in the school. Setting the canvas involves standing back and surveying the landscape with a view to making changes and using data to help you decide the scope, magnitude, and direction of new activities. This process can take several meetings and will undoubtedly involve multiple perspectives and some disagreement.

Purpose and Context

During their careers, artists paint many paintings, some that are very similar to one another and some that are very different. As educators begin the

> **Setting the Canvas**
>
> What is our purpose?
>
> What roles do we play?
>
> Who are the audiences?

process of using data for decision making, they need to think about what issue they are considering for this painting. Are they reading the vital signs of the school as a baseline for planning? If so, what areas do they want to concentrate on? What are their priorities? Where do they need to focus energy and consider making changes? Or are they examining the impact of initiatives that are already in place? If so, what was the area of focus? What was the initiative? What did they hope would result?

It is the first staff meeting of the year, and Janet has decided that the team will use the meeting to begin their school improvement planning. She has distributed a short survey to everyone on staff (including the secretaries and custodians) asking them anonymously to identify what each of them thinks is the most serious issue that the school needs to address in its improvement planning and to give their reasons for making this choice. She got a good response, with some people including more than one item. Before the meeting, Janet sorted the responses that she received into 7 categories. Here is her arrangement:

- The aging and crowded physical plant (10 mentions)
- The changing nature of the students (more diversity, second language learners, challenging home lives) (9 mentions)
- Literacy (8 mentions)
- Low number of parents coming to school events (8 mentions)
- Bullying on the playground (5 mentions)
- Not enough computers for teachers (2 mentions)
- No gymnasium (1 mention)

During the meeting, they discussed all of the issues in the categories that Janet had identified. As they talked about their issues, it became clear to Janet that some of the staff had identified things that were very personal to them but might not be critical to the school as a whole. She also noticed that the issues were all very "school-specific" and wondered if the parents would identify any others.

By the end of the meeting they had agreed that the three top issues were the aging and crowded building (without a proper gymnasium); literacy; and parental involvement, each of them with a strong lobby group supporting their choice as #1.

Roles

Although using data effectively requires collaborative planning and action, not everyone has the time or the inclination to serve as a leader. There is increasing evidence, however, that administrators cannot and should not do this work alone. Teacher leadership can be a powerful force in educational change as professional learning communities develop to tackle intransigent and difficult problems. As Katzenmeyer and Moller (2000) describe it, "Teachers who are leaders lead within and beyond the classroom, identify with and contribute to a community of teacher learners and leaders, and influence others toward improved educational practice" (p. 5).

Moving beyond mandated school improvement to genuine attention to changes in practice and in structures requires a concerted effort from teacher leaders and engagement of the school community.

As the staff meeting drew to a close, Janet began to wonder if she had done the right thing in putting this process in motion. The staff had been testier than she had expected. Their easy interaction with one another was strained. She decided to invite the three people who were the most vocal leaders (Sharon, the lead teacher of English; Dwayne, who teaches math and PE and coaches many of the teams; and, Sylvia, a relatively new teacher who is teaching a sixth-grade class and coordinating the parent volunteers) to form a "fact-finding" committee and locate as much information as they could about each of the top three issues. She asked them if they would be willing to take on this task if she and the vice principal would cover two of their classes a week for the next month so that they could gather information. They all agreed.

Assignment #4

Purpose, Context, and Roles

Every painting has a subject and a theme. Use Task Sheet #4 in the Resource section to delineate the scope and priorities for your work.

Purpose and Context

Ask each team member to identify, in writing, what she or he believes is the most pressing and compelling issue for the team to consider, with a rationale for the choice, and put it into a collection box in advance of a meeting of the team. The issue could be an area of concern that the member believes needs attention or review and monitoring of an initiative that is already in place.

Post all of the issues and rationales on the wall for the team meeting. Because you are working as a team, do not be surprised to find that different team members have identified different areas for attention.

At the meeting, each member has two minutes to describe the priority and give a rationale for this choice.

The staff members then choose their top three issues and write them on cards. Place the cards on the wall, ordered by the number of times that an issue has been nominated.

Select the three issues that have the most "votes" from the staff for further consideration and investigation.

Roles

Who are the respected teacher leaders in your group? Who will be serious about their involvement and forge relationships within the staff? Which staff members should take responsibility for developing each of the three issues more fully by conducting a "needs assessment" and bringing more information about the issue to the next meeting so that the group can make an informed choice about where they think the school should put its energy?

The first meeting of Janet's "fact-finding team" was an odd one. When it began, the staff members were almost like children playing hooky. They couldn't believe that they were actually sitting in the tiny conference room off Janet's office while she and the VP were teaching their classes. Sharon even suggested that they should maybe go and check that everything was okay. As reality took over, they realized that they had other, more pressing tasks to do. They needed to "find things out" about the H. C. Andersen building, about literacy at H. C. Andersen, and about parental involvement at H. C. Andersen so that they could recommend a single priority to the staff. And they had each already told the staff what they knew and had made their preference clear. What did Janet expect them to do?

First off, they decided to send an e-mail to the district director who was responsible for building maintenance and ask him what, if anything, was being planned for H. C. Andersen.

They spent the rest of the meeting discussing what they saw as important issues related to literacy and to parent involvement. Dwayne summed it up by saying: "Well, they are so closely interlinked; it's hard to pull them apart. Sure, our kids don't do very well on literacy tests, but what can we expect? It's the homes that they come from. Most of them don't speak English at home. Their parents don't really value school. If we could fix their home lives, they'd do better at school."

With only a few minutes left, they realized that they needed to "do" something before their next meeting. They agreed that they would also ask someone from the district to come and talk to them about the literacy test scores for H. C. Andersen students. When Sylvia suggested that they send a brief survey home to parents asking them their views about literacy and about involvement in the school, Dwayne remarked jokingly, "If they answer it, we'll know how involved they are." But they decided to do it. The parents had actually been pretty responsive to the "playground survey" that they sent home last year.

Audiences

Although it often happens in private, decision making in schools is a very public affair. Leadership teams are expected to represent the interests and perspectives of many different groups and individuals. Building and maintaining trust in a school depends on mutual obligation, trusted relationships, and local knowledge. So, like all artists, the leadership team has an audience for its work. They are not the only people who will be affected by or care about the issues that they are discussing and decisions that they are likely to make or recommend.

These audiences may include other staff members, parents, the school advisory council, the local community, even the local media. It is important for the leadership team to consider all of the various audiences while they are deciding about their focus and priorities. They might even decide to include some of the audiences in the planning process.

Within the school, it is critical for the whole staff to be aware of and engaged in the planning process. Change is hard work that requires motivation and capacity (Earl, Watson, Levin, Leithwood, Fullan, & Torrance, 2003). If the staff does not believe in the changes and are not willing to explore and use new practices, nothing really changes. They need to be part of the thinking and planning that leads to adopting innovations and new directions. Later, they must feel motivated to continue with the changes, adapting as necessary to address changing conditions. This means that considering the data becomes everyone's business and that all perspectives get "air time," even though there may be tension and disagreement.

But the staff is not the only important audience. When you are serious about using data and talking about it with your community, you need to address the issues that matter to the community, and the data have to "ring true" for them as well so that you can use the data to begin an ongoing community conversation. It is through this ongoing conversation that schools and their community come to share values and develop a shared vision for the school, and it is here that schools provide information about how they are doing (accountability) through discussion of meaningful and worthwhile data.

It is especially important in the early stages of identifying the problem to identify the various key audiences and ensure that they are engaged in thinking about the issues.

Assignment #5

Identifying Audiences

In any planning exercise, it is important to ensure that everyone who is going to be affected by the changes is not only aware of the plans but engaged in thinking about what to do. It may seem easier in the beginning for a few people to go ahead and establish the plan, but you increase the likelihood of the plan faltering or failing later.

In this assignment, use Task Sheet #5 in the Resource section to think about all of the people who are currently involved in your priority and make an audience chart to show their roles and relationships with one another. Be specific.

In each rectangle, use names, describe responsibilities, and use arrows to link the people in their working relationships.

(Continued)

> Around the outside of the chart (in the circles), list all of the people who might be affected by this plan and need to be brought on board.
>
> Beside each circle with a group or individual's name, describe what you will do to engage them in the process and keep them informed along the way.

When you know who needs to be involved, you can ensure that they are all at least informed and even engaged in the planning.

PLANNING THIS PICTURE

The next stage in the process of painting data pictures relates to planning. We believe that it is very important to spend time early in the process thinking about the problem, identifying the issues, and getting clear about what is already known. This chapter details a planning process based on what leaders know already and on where they want to go with their schools.

> **Planning This Picture**
>
> What do we *think* we know?
>
> Where do we want to go?

Historically, schools have defined their goals, and teachers have taken individual responsibility for their part in student learning. The new world view that we described in Chapter 2 shows how critical it is for schools to be responsive to many forces both inside and outside their immediate community. Serving all students well requires a concerted and collective effort. Educators need to see themselves as part of a larger professional community, with responsibility for all of the young people in their school, not just the ones that they see in their classes. This requires planning. Educational leaders need to look at the future, understand where they are now, imagine the hoped for future, and work with educators to devise the strategies that need to be set in place to get there.

A Vision of Your Future

Hedley Beare, an Australian futurist, has devised a framework for thinking about futures that can be very useful for educators (Beare, 2001). He identifies three kinds of futures: possible futures, probable futures, and preferable futures. As he describes it, "planning is a timetable for taking deliberate actions to maximize the chance of achieving your preferred futures, a kind of road map to guide you into a future of your own making" (p. 102).

This simple but powerful process provides a mechanism for building a vision, for charting where you think you are now, and for deciding where you want to go. The gap between the probable and the preferable future points to priority area(s) for change and to places where you can focus investigation and monitor progress of your actions in reducing the gap between current state of affairs and the preferred future.

When you identify your preferable futures you are really developing a vision for change—a picture of what you want to accomplish and bring into existence. Vision, as we know, is one of the key ingredients of effective schools. Plans provide the road map of strategies to carry the vision into reality—to chart the course towards your preferred future.

Possible Futures: Futures that could happen, some of which are likely; most are unlikely.

Probable Futures: Futures that will probably happen, unless something happens to throw them off course.

Preferable Futures: Futures that you prefer to have happen and that you will plan to make happen out of the possible and probable futures.
—Beare (2001)

While the responses to their requests to central office and the survey to parents were coming in, Janet and the planning team at H. C. Andersen School started to think about their literacy focus and realized that they had a very sketchy image of their intentions. They knew that they wanted to improve their graduates' literacy but they didn't have an image of what that would mean. They decided to use a portion of a staff meeting to "chart their futures."

POSSIBLE FUTURES

As a starting point, they used the "wall" technique to brainstorm all of the things that might happen at H. C. Andersen Middle School that could be related to literacy. All staff members spent some time writing their ideas on cards and posting them on the wall. Then the whole staff worked to group the ideas into categories. They were surprised by the range of ideas that emerged when they described the possible futures but were fascinated by how they grouped into categories. They called one major category "Our Kids." It focused on the kinds of students that came to the school. Who were they? What was their background? The issue of diversity among the students surfaced again. This led them to a discussion of the neighborhood and whether or not it would change in the near future. They speculated about federal immigration policies. They mused about some segments of the school society moving to another area of the city. One of the teachers had heard that a new subdivision was being planned, and the custodian (who lived in the area) mentioned that quite a few older residents were considering selling their homes and moving into smaller dwellings (townhouses or apartments). Maybe the demographics of the school would shift in the future.

Another category focused on "Programs." They talked about the possibility of the district housing a special program at H. C. Andersen for young adolescents who were capable but not succeeding in regular classes. The school might also be designated a community school and be open for use by other agencies and groups after hours. The adolescent program would result in a slight increase in enrollment but it would also mean the addition of two staff members. Being a community school would mean sharing space and negotiating connections with a range of other groups.

Also within the "Programs" category, the group talked about the nature of their literacy programs at H. C. Andersen. There was some gentle discussion about the lack of coordination among the teachers in relation to literacy, and someone offered a possibility that the staff could work as a whole to devise a literacy strategy that connected the world of their students to the curriculum.

These discussions led them to the realization that some key staff members were likely to retire in the next few years, and they would lose a lot of valuable expertise.

The rambling and productive discussion resulted in the following concept map:

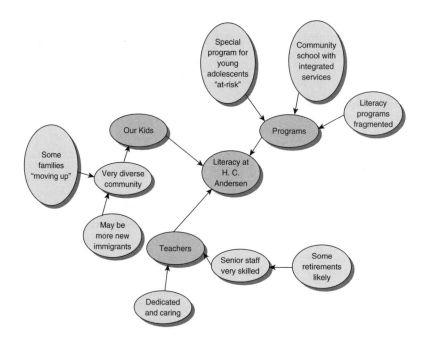

PROBABLE FUTURES

When it came to probable futures, the staff really focused on the issue of literacy. They started by describing the current state of affairs in literacy and then went through an exercise of anticipating what literacy would "look like" if they didn't intervene or change anything. They realized early on that they shouldn't look at literacy in isolation because a number of factors were related to literacy: student language at home; parental support for literacy; teacher qualifications and experience; student achievement, student attitudes, and engagement; programs; school culture; even the physical plant.

As they proceeded, they found that they had a good deal of information from the district about their students' literacy test scores. They also had their own informal knowledge of the school community and how the school operated. Here is what they thought they knew about the school:

- Many of the students in the school were new immigrants.
- The school had been experiencing declining enrollment over the past three years.
- Approximately 30% of students did not meet the literacy standard on the most recent state test, and they were not reaching their annual yearly progress targets.
- Parents were respectful of the school, attended events, and responded to requests from the school but did not initiate contact.
- Although staffing had been stable for many years, this was starting to shift from an experienced staff to a new group of less experienced teachers.
- Teachers tended to have expertise with a particular grade because of experience in that grade and many of them had specific subject strengths (art, music, PE), but there were no cross-curricular programs in the school, and staff members tended to work as individuals, focusing on their own grade and subject areas.
- The library was well stocked, and the teacher-librarian was willing to provide support programs, but the library was not well used, and very few students actually signed books out to read.
- The physical plant was laid out in wings that made it hard for teachers of different grades to work together.

It became clear that if the trends continued into the future there might be reason for concern. The group members described H. C. Andersen this way in their scenario:

Literacy learning at H. C. Andersen may become a problem. The probable future, if we do nothing to intervene, is that some of our students will do very well because they have many family resources available to them; however, some of the students will continue to struggle with literacy. Those who do not perform very well on the state literacy assessment will not become proficient readers and writers. This will limit their access to future educational opportunities and will keep them in a state of under-privilege and likely poverty.

Although the school has a strong reputation for sports and for caring teachers, it already has a declining enrollment, and its reputation is likely to suffer unless it is also seen to be serving students well academically.

PREFERABLE FUTURE

Then the group members brainstormed what H. C. Andersen would be like in their preferable future. Here is their list:

In our preferable future, H. C. Andersen School:
- ensures that students develop the knowledge, skills, and values needed to be successful in a rapidly changing world.
- is a strong, vibrant school.
- has a professional culture of cooperation among staff.
- is a caring and interesting place to be.

They also identified their image of literacy teaching and learning:

In H. C. Andersen's preferable future:
- all students are competent readers, writers, speakers, and listeners.
- students enjoy literacy and choose literacy activities independently for pleasure.
- parents and the community support literacy development formally and informally.

The "fact-finding" group asked if they could continue as a small subcommittee, at least for a while, to think about what else they needed to know in order to make schoolwide improvement plans.

Before educators can make any reasonable predictions about the future, they need to know what the present is like. This is one place where appealing to data becomes important. Charting your future involves asking questions and examining your context from multiple perspectives. You can begin this process by thinking about data that you have available to describe the present state of affairs before predicting what things will be like without intervention (probable) and imagining what you would like the future to be (preferable).

Assignment #6

Charting Your Futures

Charting the future involves determining *what you know* about your school and thinking about *where you want to go* as a school. What you know about your school describes the present state of affairs. And, if nothing changes, the present state of affairs becomes your probable future. In contrast, your preferable future is intentional and improvement oriented; it is what you want to plan to happen.

Ultimately, the goal is for your probable and preferred futures to be one in the same.

Think about your situation and the area for attention that you identified and about what you know, or think you know already, about the school in relation to this priority. Use Task Sheet #6 in the Resource section to record your deliberations.

Possible Futures

First open your minds and do a far-reaching brainstorm. What are the possible futures? What factors could change in your context? Imagine all the possibilities, no matter how unlikely. What if the demography of the school changed dramatically? What if the district amalgamated with a neighboring one? What if key staff members retired or moved? This is the time for letting your imagination take over and speculating about things that "could happen," even if they do not seem likely right now. Think about the factors that are likely to be important in your future scenario, things like student achievement, school culture, student demographics, student attitudes and engagement, teacher demographics, teaching and assessment practices, parent involvement, and programs, and use these headings to stimulate your discussion.

Create concept maps of the "possible scenarios" that you come up with.

Probable Futures

The next step is more sobering. What is the probable future? What will happen in your scenario if nothing changes and no one intervenes? Using the same categories that you defined in the concept maps, describe, in as much detail as you can from your first-hand knowledge and from available data, what your school is like right now. Then make some predictions about what it will look like in the not-too-distant future if nothing changes, if you do nothing differently than you are doing now. What do you think you know already? What is the current state of affairs? What are the trends that are likely to continue? What would you predict, based on your current knowledge, about the probable future?

Preferable Futures

Finally, you are ready to imagine your preferable future. What would you like the future to be like? What would be similar and different from the probable future? Describe, in as much detail as you can, your desired image for your school, what you would like it to be.

(Continued)

> Again, think in terms of categories like student achievement, school culture, student demographics, student attitudes and engagement, teacher demographics, teaching and assessment practices, parent involvement, and programs. Write a scenario to describe the school that you hope to become.

Although you may already know a good deal about your school, there is always more to find out, and more information may often mean making adjustments to earlier decisions. There is always another way to look at an issue. Data provide new lenses for thinking and make room for challenging our existing beliefs. Even before you can start planning, it is important to consider data to confirm that the priorities that you have identified are actually the ones that deserve serious attention.

When Janet met with the "fact-finders," she was delighted that they were getting information from the district office and from parents. The sub-committee had already had some input, and they would be reporting back to the whole staff at a staff meeting, so all of the obvious groups were included.

When the "fact-finders" addressed the staff at their next meeting, they had lots to report.

First, they had a memo from the district office telling them that H. C. Andersen was scheduled for a building "refit" the next year. The news would be made public at the next meeting of the Board of Trustees, and someone from the school would be invited to sit on the planning committee to decide what would be done.

Their meeting with the literacy consultant had been really interesting. She drew attention to the fact that, although H. C. Andersen students as a group were about average in the district on the state literacy assessment, there were some unusual distributions of scores. Their scores fluctuated from year to year, with what appeared to be differences across cohorts of students. The literacy survey from the statewide assessment showed that the students liked reading better than writing. Mostly girls were doing better than boys. The staff had seen these data before, but they still weren't sure what it meant. They agreed to spend some time thinking about it.

The literacy consultant also told them that there was a person at the district office who would do additional analyses of the test data if they wanted to know more.

The survey that the fact-finders sent home to parents was short and sweet. They only asked two questions:

> What do you think the top 3 priorities for improvement should be at H. C. Andersen this year?

> What could H. C. Andersen do to make you feel involved in the school?

They were pleased and surprised when they got back answers from about 60% of the parents. And the results were fascinating.

- 80% of the respondents indicated that ensuring students learned to read and write was among the top 3 priorities.
- 70% mentioned something about keeping students interested in school (relevance, interesting courses, activities that kids like to do, making my kid like school).
- 30% said "help my children feel good about themselves."
- 25% said "get the students ready for high school."
- 20% mentioned safety in the school yard and to and from school.
- There were a few topics that only came from one or two people, and no one mentioned the physical building.

When it came to involving parents, 45% of the respondents said that they felt like they were involved already. Many of them made suggestions about ways to enhance involvement: "parent interviews spread over afternoons and evenings for a whole week; having parent/child meetings about different subjects to help parents help their children with homework; inviting parents to talk about their jobs and experiences." One even said "Invite us for tea."

The staff meeting discussion was lively. It did not take long before someone said, "Well, it's pretty clear to me that we have to focus on literacy. It's one of the highest priorities for the parents, and there is going to be a 'refit' so we can stop worrying about the building. Hey, if one of us is on the 'refit' committee, we can even make sure that the changes to the building are consistent with what we decide to do in literacy."

Janet was interested to see that the "fact-finding" group was very engaged in the discussion and that they were the ones who kept coming back to the information that they had collected. She was not surprised when they volunteered to continue to work with her as a planning committee, at least for a while. They agreed to meet later in the week to decide what to do next.

Assignment #7

Initial Environmental Scan

Planning activities do not begin on a clean slate. They emerge from existing and sometimes longstanding issues that have been avoided or ignored. "Setting the canvas" includes identifying the

(Continued)

top issues for consideration and then verifying that you are heading in the right direction by confirming the direction with the pertinent audiences. Although your initial decisions may well change as time goes on, the group needs to start with an idea of the priorities for attention and become familiar with the actual state of affairs, not just the opinions of a few individuals.

Think about the top three issues that you identified earlier. What do you know about them? What is the current state of affairs? What data do you have that can help you think about your priorities? How could you find out more?

Use Task Sheet #7 in the Resource section and do an environmental scan to gather data about your top priority and report your findings back to the group.

Becoming Data Literate

We often find ourselves in groups of educators who proclaim that they cannot do this "data stuff" because they are no good with math. Although we think this is a sad indictment of the math phobia that seems to plague our society, we want to reassure all of you, as readers, that you do not need to be mathematics wizards to be "data literate." Data literacy is not the same as "crunching numbers." It is certainly important for school leaders to have a basic working knowledge of how "numbers work" and about what measurement and statistical concepts mean, but they do not need to become statisticians; they need to be data literate. Data literacy refers to a thinking process—a process of:

- standing back and deciding what you need to know and why,
- collecting or locating the necessary data,
- finding ways to link key data sources,
- ensuring that the data are worth considering,
- being aware of their limitations,
- thinking about what the results mean, and finally,
- systematically considering an issue from a range of perspectives so that you really feel that you have evidence to explain, support, and also challenge your point of view.

In the beginning, using data may feel like a complicated and time-consuming process, and there is considerable evidence that many school leaders are not yet equipped to use data. But these are not good reasons to avoid data. In fact, schools are complicated places that deserve to be represented in all their complexity and not reduced to "stick figures."

In this chapter we describe a process for becoming data literate, with examples from H. C. Andersen, as the staff progress through the process of engaging with data in their pursuit of better decisions. We have included actual data from the school. Although that makes the chapter rather long, we hope that you will spend some time looking at the details of their data and trying to see what they see (and even perhaps things they do not see), so that you actually live the experience through their eyes before you start with your own data.

BLOCKING THE CANVAS

> **Blocking the Canvas**
>
> What do we want (or need) to know?
>
> What data do we need?
>
> How good are these data?

Often there is the tendency among people in schools to jump too quickly into the data. The risk involved in this practice is that you can end up caring about something because it is easy to measure, rather than first caring about something because it is part of your preferred future and *then* deciding how to measure it. Using data for school improvement planning does not begin with the data you have. Instead, it begins with thinking about what you want (or need) to know and deciding what data you require to answer your questions. This stage of the process involves thinking and hypothesizing about what forces are at work in relation to your priority and your context. It is a time of talking about what you think is going on and of making your tacit knowledge visible so that you can see what you, individually and as a group, "believe to be true." Sometimes this process is emotionally hard, as people discover that they actually have very different views and beliefs about issues of practice that are often close to their hearts. Nevertheless, this process of making your "taken for granted" ideas explicit is exactly what has to happen so that you can have a basis for deciding what data you need and establishing the hypotheses that will guide your thinking. Then you can collect or locate the best data for your purpose.

What Do We Want to Know?

When it comes to using data for decision making in schools, the hardest part is asking the right questions. Why? Because the right questions are the ones that we are least likely to put forward; the ones that challenge our "taken for granted" views of our professional life and make us most vulnerable. Going deeper in understanding what is happening in any school comes from challenging what "we believe to be true" and taking an honest look at the way things are. As Hargreaves and Fullan (1998) said:

> In a changing world, a healthy school is one where teachers constantly revisit and renew their purposes; always looking for evidence and feedback about how well they are doing, and honestly examining whether they need to do things differently or better. (p. 30)

Most of us are comfortable asking questions that have positive or confirming answers and support our existing practices. It is a lot tougher to ask questions that might highlight negative or uncomfortable answers that challenge us to change. But that is exactly what has to happen. Sometimes the most compelling questions arise out of educators' discussions about what is happening at their school—when they talk about and conjecture about questions such as: How are we doing? Are we serving all of the students well? What are our relative strengths and weaknesses? Why are things the way they are? What factors contribute to our situation? But the discussion does not end with the self-proclaimed answers. Instead each idea should become a hypothesis that can be investigated and examined by considering data. This is the first stage of the "accountability conversation"—saying out loud what you believe and live by in your work so that you can examine it. And, because it is hard, this conversation can take a good deal of time. Guard against ending it too soon or staying on the surface with issues that may be interesting but are not controversial.

When the planning group met again they found themselves at an early impasse. Sharon, who had been the original literacy champion in the group, came to the meeting with a plan. She was sure that the school should adopt a program that she had heard about at a literacy "in-service." The program focused on adolescent literacy, and all they needed to do was send three people to a professional development session and buy the materials. Then they could start implementing it.

The other planning group members balked. "Why would we spend all that money and commit the school to a major program shift right now? We're just beginning to get a feel for the problems. How can you be so sure that this is the right solution?"

After a few tense moments, Sharon agreed that maybe she was being hasty and perhaps they should spend a little more time thinking about the problem before charging ahead.

The group decided to review their initial scan of data. They found that they knew a lot about their school already and about factors that might be associated with literacy. At least they knew enough to establish that improving literacy for their students was likely to be a multifaceted and complicated undertaking. They knew that the language backgrounds for their kids were very mixed. They also realized that the staff got along well but they didn't do much work together, except for coaching team sports.

All of this information was interesting but it didn't hang together. There were a lot of gaps and holes.

Janet took a chance and asked the question: Why do you think we have the literacy profile that we have? Initially discussion focused on what the profile actually was. Everyone agreed that there was a need to focus on literacy. But there was considerable disagreement about who needed help with literacy. It wasn't at all clear from the data which students they should be paying attention to. It looked like boys were having trouble, and the students liked reading better than writing.

Sylvia was quick to focus on the boys. "Don't forget, we have a bunch of young boys in the seventh-grade cohort. They are always slower than the others. I worry that they're pretty disenchanted and are getting turned off school pretty early. Maybe we should start a 'boys' group' to talk about what they could do instead of hanging out at the mall."

Dwayne looked annoyed and suggested that the problem students were the ones from the "new" families who weren't very good at school work. "We don't need a 'boys' group.' That's why having sports teams is so important. At least they can do well at something."

Sharon reminded them that there was no schoolwide literacy program and, as an English teacher, she was well aware that the English department was the group who ended up having responsibility for language development. "We could probably do a lot better if we made it a priority and worked together. I don't even know what literacy activities the rest of you do in your classes."

Not to be outdone, Sylvia added, "Well, if the parents were more involved in homework, I'm sure that literacy would be better."

Janet kept steering the discussion back to her original question about the reasons for their literacy profile and reminding them that they were not making decisions today—just exploring ideas and possibilities and deciding what else they needed to know.

Emotions were high throughout the discussion, but over time the planning group identified a wide range of possible areas for investigation. As they talked, it became more obvious to Janet that they needed more, and more focused, information before they could move ahead. It was time to formalize the planning process. She recapped the discussion by saying, "Wow, we've gone through a lot of ideas. So far it seems to me that we have talked about the influences of student characteristics like age and gender and home background, and about the kind of family involvement there is in kids doing homework, and about the kinds of programs and teaching strategies that we are using. I'd like to take some time and see if I can pull this all together before the next meeting." She ended the meeting by asking each member to think about committing to continuing as part of the planning committee for the remainder of the year. They would work with her to take the whole staff through a process of deciding what to do and then turning their plans into action, using evidence to inform their work along the way.

The ideas that come from discussion of the priority start to delineate the composition of the painting that will result by defining the categories of interest, or the colors that the artist needs to include to paint this picture. The following figure is an artist's palette with each color representing an indicator category. Just as artists choose the colors that they need to paint their picture with all its subtleties and contrasts, school teams must choose the indicator categories that describe their school and their priority realistically, in all its complexity. The indicators come from making their beliefs explicit and then investigating them as hypotheses, not as "givens." Other categories emerge as educators think about their own contexts and what they need to know.

What Indicator Categories?

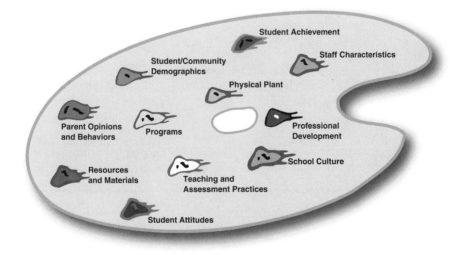

Indicator categories give an initial organizer for deciding what data might be useful in the long run. When school teams spend time thinking about the categories of indicators that make sense in their situation, they are much more likely to have a clear picture of what they need to know to help them in their planning.

Indicator Categories And Some Possible Uses

Category	Definition	Examples of Possible Uses; Questions You Might Ask
Student/Community Demographics	Statistical characteristics of human populations.	Who are the school's clients? What is the school's context? What are the past demographic trends? What are the likely future demographics?
Student Achievement	What students know and are able to do.	How well do our students perform? Are all of our students learning? Are students performing differently on one type of test versus another type? What are the learning profiles for our students?
Teaching and Assessment Practices	Educational events and practices occurring in the classroom. What educators do in their classrooms in instruction and assessment.	What teaching and assessment strategies are we using? What teaching strategies are related to the desired school and classroom results? How might we change our teaching and assessment practices to achieve the desired results?
Parent Opinion and Behaviors	How parents feel about and interact with the school. How parents support their children.	What are the views of the community? How well are we connecting with the parent community? What are the relationships of parent and home conditions with school factors?
School Culture	The assumptions, beliefs, and relationships that define the organization's view of itself and its environment.	What does the staff of this school believe about student learning, athletic achievements, discipline, etc.? What is the nature of the professional relationships? What are the central foci of the school?
Student Attitudes	Descriptions of how students feel about . . .	How engaged are students in this school?

Category	Definition	*Examples of Possible Uses; Questions You Might Ask*
Staff Characteristics	Descriptive information about the faculty.	What credentials and talents do staff members hold? How are different faculty strengths being utilized in the school? What are the ages, backgrounds, and interests of the staff?
Programs	Descriptions and course outlines that provide information about intended and delivered curriculum.	What programs do we offer? What patterns of programs are students taking? Which courses are most challenging for students?
Resources and Materials	Resources and materials to support program and instruction.	What materials are teachers actually using in their classrooms? What resources would be used that are not available?
Physical Plant	Facilities, equipment, and physical spaces.	What are the patterns of use for facilities and equipment in the school?
Professional Development	Activities that teachers engage in to become better teachers.	What professional development activities are available to our teachers? What professional development activities have teachers participated in?

Assignment #8

Selecting Your Colors

Before you ever think about the data that you need, you must set the stage by being clear about what you think you know already in relation to your priority and use both existing data and your "tacit" knowledge to map the terrain.

This is a challenging task, so decide who is going to facilitate the process and keep the group on task. This needs to be someone who is trusted and seen to be impartial and fair. Use Task Sheet #8 in the Resource section as a guide.

(Continued)

As a group, think about your priority. What information do you have already that gives you some ideas about what is going on? What else do you think you know that is pertinent? What do you think is happening? How would you explain the situation?

Remember, this task requires you to share what you are thinking and put it forward for examination and challenge. Take the time that is required for the conversation to go in as many directions as it needs to, without avoiding touchy issues, being caught in premature closure, or getting sidetracked from the priority.

Have someone keep a running record of the ideas that emerge.

Categorize the ideas using the color palette to map your indicators. At the same time, for each category (color) ask yourself if there is anything that you *think you already know* about your priority with respect to that category. For example, if literacy improvement is your priority and you are dealing with parent involvement as a category, ask yourself what you know about parent involvement in your school as it pertains to literacy improvement. For some of the colors you will have lots to say, for others not quite as much. In much the same way, Monet's images of Giverny were predominately green, but there were hints of other colors as well.

Review the categories on the color palette and think about what additional information might be useful. Do not worry about what data you will need. Focus on the areas that may be pertinent and how you think they might influence your priority.

What Data Do We Need?

When the leadership team has identified the areas where they need information, they can start to look for the best data to help them make better sense of the situation. Most districts and schools collect lots of information and are beginning to organize and store it in ways that make it more accessible and to connect data from different sources. Many have given students unique identification numbers that make tracking and linking data easier, and most have electronic data systems and software that allow schools to gather, organize, and aggregate data for their own purposes. Remember, data can be much more than numbers. Opinions, anecdotes, and observations are all acceptable as data if they come from defensible sources and are supported by other information. Once they start looking, schools will find that they have lots of data available. The trick is to identify and locate the data that will be most useful to them in their planning. The search is on for the data that tells them the most and *tells their story the best;* not the best story, but the best depiction of their reality. The key to linking data categories to actual data sources is for staff to be clear about the questions that they are asking so that the data can be organized and processed to address them.

Certainly the most important data for making deep improvements is data about students' performance. Supovitz and Klein (2003) described three different kinds of assessment data that give schools a focal point for action.

Using Student Performance Data for Improvement	
Performance Data	*Use for Improvement*
External Assessments (National, State/Provincial)	Provide initial direction. Identify early topics for professional development. Identify students in need of additional support. Set long-term goals. Sometimes celebration.
Schoolwide Assessments	Refine instructional strategies based on detailed feedback. Adjust professional development strategies. Refine and hone assistance plans for individual students. Allow faculty to inquire together about the relationships between teaching practices and student learning.
Classroom Assessments	Provide precise, tailored, and flexible data available to teachers to guide their individualized practices.

SOURCE: Adapted from Supovitz and Klein, 2003.

But student performance data, on their own, only give part of the picture. All of the other categories provide lenses for understanding and investigating student learning. The following table gives examples of data that can be useful in helping to understand the complexities and intricacies of the reality of schools.

Examples of Possible Data Within Indicator Categories	
Category	*Example of Data or Data Sources*
Student Demographics	Attendance Enrollment Grade level Ethnicity Gender First language Health issues Socioeconomic status
Student Achievement	Standardized, norm-referenced, and criterion-referenced tests Questioning in class Performance- and standards-based assessments

(Continued)

Examples of Possible Data Within Indicator Categories	
Category	*Example of Data or Data Sources*
	Teacher-made tests, projects, quizzes
	Teachers' observations
	Grades and grade point averages
Teaching and Assessment Practices	Instructional and learning strategies
	Instructional time and environment
	Organization of instructional components
	Assessment practices
	Classroom management philosophies
Parent Opinions and Behaviors	Parent perceptions
	Parent involvement in the school
	Parent support of student learning
School Culture	Relationships among educators
	Relationships among students and educators
	Beliefs about learning and teaching
Staff Demographics	Background
	Interests
	Qualifications
	Gender
	Ethnicity
	Attendance
Programs	Program descriptions
	Course outlines
	Special programs
Resources and Materials	Computers
	Textbooks
	Software
	Workbooks
	Art supplies
	Musical instruments
Physical Plant	Configuration of space
	Playground

> A critical friend is "a trusted person who asks provocative questions, provides data to be examined through another lens, and offers critique of a person's work, as a friend."
> —Costa and Kallick (1995)

This is a point in the process at which it may be valuable to call on a "critical friend" to help with the technical aspects of locating, organizing, and analyzing the data and to facilitate the work of the group.

Look for someone who not only understands how to work with data but who will also be respectful of your process and work with you to find the data that you need, not just summarize the data that they have.

At the next staff meeting, Janet and the planning team shared their thinking to date. Janet had summarized their last planning team meeting into a set of questions that the committee agreed they wanted to pursue further:

- Which students are doing well in relation to literacy, and which ones are having difficulty?
- Are there differences in literacy related to student, family, and school characteristics, specifically gender, attendance, participation in sports, family circumstances, educational history, grade, homework?
- What kinds of literacy problems are the students having?
- What literacy teaching and assessment strategies appear to be most effective with middle school kids?

Janet also invited two guests to meet the staff. One of them was Jason, the data specialist from the district, who had agreed to help them get access to district data and to do the analyses that they wanted. Janet had hoped that he would also be able to facilitate their discussion, but he was already overburdened with his data job and seemed much more comfortable with numbers than with people. So Janet had also invited Thomas, a retired superintendent from a neighboring district. Janet had met him when they took a leadership course together. She was hoping that the staff would agree to have Thomas work with them as a facilitator so that she could participate in the discussions. She had been bold enough to go to her superintendent and ask that the district hire Thomas as a consultant to work with her.

The staff was interested in the progress of the planning committee, and no one seemed to object to having the two "critical friends" working with them. They agreed that they would all work to cover classes so that the planning team could meet regularly.

When the planning committee met again, Jason and Thomas joined them. Janet asked Thomas if he would chair. The planning group was more subdued than usual, so when Thomas asked where they thought they should start, Janet began by asking Jason what data he thought might be relevant to their preliminary questions.

He suggested that he could do some more detailed analyses of state assessment data for H. C. Andersen School. He also offered to look at data about attendance and language in the home that the district kept.

At that point, Sharon mentioned that every student who enters H. C. Andersen is given an informal reading and writing inventory. "It's not very sophisticated. We created it from some materials that the district distributed a few years ago, with some leveled exemplars of student work. It gives us some ideas about where to start in grouping students for instruction. Maybe it would be worth looking at."

Dwayne was really interested in finding out how the H. C. Andersen students were doing when they went on to high school. He offered to contact the guidance counselor to see what he could find out. Janet wondered if he was thinking about the students who were really active in sports.

Sylvia wondered aloud whether the school council had any data about the families in the school. She knew a little from her contact with the volunteer parents, but that didn't seem very scientific. Maybe she would do some sleuthing before the next meeting.

Janet said that she would spend some time before the next meeting looking at literature about instruction and assessment in literacy for the team to look at as well. Sharon looked surprised but didn't say anything.

So far Thomas was having an easy time. He had kept notes of the tasks that they were each going to do before the next meeting, and they set a date to meet again.

Assignment #9

From Indicator Categories to Data Sources

This assignment takes you from the broad indicator categories that you have identified as pertinent to investigating your priority to finding the best data sources in the morass of data that are available in your school and your district. This means turning the conjecture and hypotheses in the earlier session into actual questions that you want to try to illuminate using data. Use Task Sheet #9 in the Resource section to record your deliberations.

Assign each color on the palette that you developed to a group of two or three. Each group's task is to revisit the discussion about that indicator category and turn the ideas that were generated into questions that might be considered by appealing to data.

For each of the indicator categories (colors), ask yourself what sources of *evidence* you could appeal to in order to confirm or challenge what you think you know about your priority. Some sources of evidence, because of their composition, will appeal to more than one category. For each question, start making a list of the data that you can utilize or that you need to collect, with a description of the type of data and how you get access to it. Then go exploring to find out what pertinent data may be available so that you only actually collect data that you really need and cannot get elsewhere.

How Good Are These Data?

Many different types of data are available to educators, but not all data are high quality. This makes it important to consider the various sources of data and determine their value and appropriateness for the purpose at hand. When data result from procedures that are public and transparent, they can be independently considered and verified. In technical terms, judging quality means assuring reliability and validity of the interpretation of the data and identifying reference points for interpretation.

Using data requires some understanding of the principles of measurement, although not the technical dimensions. When data are used to make decisions about students' learning and about schools, the decision makers need to be confident that their interpretations and uses of the information are credible and defensible.

Reliability

Reliability addresses the following questions: How sure are we? How confident are we that these data provide enough consistent and stable information to allow us to make statements about it with certainty? When you are using data, you are making inferences about what you know and might do from the evidence that is available to you. If you are unsure or wonder about whether your judgments could be compromised by inconsistencies or problems with the data, there is a question about reliability, and you need to take this into consideration in your interpretation.

Validity

Validity refers to accuracy of the interpretation and use of the data and answers the following questions: How well does the data measure what we are trying to understand? Does the interpretation of the data lead to appropriate conclusions and consequences? The focus in validity is on the inferences that are drawn and the consequences of these inferences. When the interpretation of any data does not reflect what was actually being measured, people can come to inaccurate conclusions.

Reference Points

Any kind of measurement refers to reference points in order to interpret the results. When carpenters measure distance, they use feet and inches. Meteorologists refer to temperature in relation to the freezing point of water ($0°$ C.) Restaurant reviewers rate the food in restaurants based on quality, originality, presentation, etc. In education the reference points fall into three categories:

- in relation to the performance of other people in a defined group (norm-referenced).
- in relation to some predetermined criteria, outcomes, or expectation (criteria- or outcomes-referenced).
- in relation to progress or performance at a prior time (self-referenced).

Reference points are used to make sense of any new data, and it is important to identify which reference point(s) are being used in interpreting information.

After school teams identify all of the data sources, they need a systematic process for considering the data quality—one that pays attention to the measurement issues and to the hypotheses that they are considering.

There was a buzz of excitement at the next planning committee meeting. Thomas remarked that he felt like he was coordinating "show and tell" as all of the team members arrived with the material that they were bringing for discussion. He started the meeting with a chart that showed the questions that they had identified, along with some of the hypotheses that had been put forward and a list of the items that the planning group had to share, so that the staff could see the magnitude of the task for the meeting. It was a good move. They had a lot to look at.

Literacy at H. C. Andersen: Questions and Hypotheses

Preliminary Questions	Hypotheses
Which students are doing well in relation to literacy, and which ones are having difficulty? Are there differences in literacy related to student, family, and school characteristics, specifically gender, attendance, participation in sports, family circumstances, educational history, grade, homework?	There is a group of young boys who are having problems. Students who come from "new" populations are less familiar with English and have trouble with language skills. Students would do better if parents helped them with homework.
What kinds of literacy problems are the students having?	Students at H. C. Andersen might have identifiable patterns of confusion or difficulty in literacy that could be targeted for remediation. Students from H. C. Andersen do fine when they get to high school.
What literacy teaching and assessment strategies appear to be most effective with middle school kids?	A schoolwide focus on literacy, with different kinds of instruction in all classes, would enhance reading and writing.

When a school team is looking for available data, they may find that it exists in a range of places and forms. State and district assessments are the obvious sources, but schools have lots of other data that they can draw on. Sometimes it is quantitative, sometimes qualitative; sometimes it is even anecdotal. The trick is to find data that are relevant to your priorities and are credible.

The H. C. Andersen team had identified a number of data elements for consideration:

- Statewide literacy assessment disaggregated by gender, age, etc.
- Student attitudes towards literacy.
- Absences from school.
- Language in the home.
- Patterns in literacy learning.
- Success in high school.

After the potential data are located come the initial investigation and quality considerations, to decide how much attention each data source deserves.

To prepare for the meeting, Thomas had gone to the university to talk to some faculty members and do some research to brush up on his knowledge about making sense of data.

As a result of his investigation, Thomas had alerted each committee member that he wanted them to describe the data that they had located at the meeting but not to jump to conclusions yet about what it might mean or what they should be doing as a result of the information. Instead, he asked them to give their opinions about the quality of the data. He asked them to explain how much confidence they had in the data: whether it addressed the pertinent issues for their decisions, whether it was detailed enough, and what reservations they might have about it. He asked Jason to start. Jason had brought data from the statewide assessments, attendance data, and data about language used in the home.

STATEWIDE ASSESSMENTS

Jason showed them several new reports that he had produced. He had summarized assessment data by gender for the past two years for H. C. Andersen, with district and state comparisons.

Jason had been surprised when Thomas asked him to question the quality of the state assessment data. But he had gone to the technical manual that came with the results and found several cautions related to disaggregated data. The one that caught his eye was that for any group smaller than 40 students, the data should not be considered reliable. He did a count of students in each gender by grade group and added it to the chart to show that there were enough students in each group. He didn't do the analysis by "disadvantage" (using free school meals data) that he had intended though, because the numbers got to be pretty small in some of those groups, and he was afraid that they would be misleading. He also realized that the reference points for interpreting this assessment were the state and district levels, but there were also internal patterns based on groups of students as they moved through the grades.

ATTENDANCE DATA

Jason had also brought reports of average daily attendance for H. C. Andersen, the state, and the district, calculated for a school by dividing the average number of students in ADA (average daily attendance) by the average number of students enrolled. Jason brought this information disaggregated by gender, but he was pretty sure that these statistics wouldn't give the staff much information, so he downloaded the attendance records from the school for the last year. This file was much more specific with data about class absences as well as daily ones. He was able to link the absence records to the student data system and do some analyses to show patterns of attendance for boys and girls in each grade. He did a quick analysis of attendance by days of the week for a ten-week period.

When it came to this attendance data, Jason thought it was pretty interesting, but he pointed out that he was skeptical because he wasn't sure how well the records were kept at the school. This comment generated laughter around the table. "You're right. It might not be too good. We don't always get the sheets to the office in time and if kids arrive late, the sheets may not get changed. I don't know if we should put too much faith in the records." Finally, Jason had some census data about the percentage of homes where English is not the first language.

LANGUAGE IN THE HOME

Because the data about language in the home came from the census, Jason felt pretty confident about it, but it was already four years old so maybe not very true to the current situation.

Jason ended his statement with a caution that had occurred to him during the week. Even though he had shown them data on attendance and language in the home, he wasn't able to connect these files to the assessment results. He reminded them not to jump to conclusions about relationships between the data sets without more analysis and never to claim that there are causal relationships.

Sometimes other agencies or organizations have data that may be useful to schools. Having good working relationships with other groups helps schools stay informed about what is available and about how to get access without violating any confidence agreements. As with all other data, it is important to know how and why the data were collected and analyzed in order to judge the quality and utility for the purpose.

COMMUNITY SURVEY OF NEEDS

Sylvia had located information through the local community services office. They kept records of all of the families who received public assistance, giving information about who lived in each home and about the range of services that they received. The information was confidential but the district might be able to get it for them. She didn't know anything about the quality of the data at this point.

Community services had also done a community survey earlier that year to determine the services and programs needed to enhance the quality of life in the community. She had a copy of the report and it included information about the way the sample was selected and how the data were analyzed. Although the sample was selected to give results of ±3, 19 times out of 20, the return rate from community members was only 45%, so the authors indicated that the results should be interpreted with some caution.

Sylvia wasn't sure how to use this information, but she said it made her realize that they needed to think more about what data they can use.

Sometimes schools already have very valuable data that they have not really paid attention to. Data that are collected by single departments or for administrative reasons can often contribute a great deal to thinking in other areas and by other people.

INFORMAL READING AND WRITING ASSESSMENTS (SIXTH GRADERS)

Sharon had done summaries of the informal reading and writing assessments for the entering students over the past four years, showing how many were judged to be "struggling" in each area that the English teachers felt they needed to do remedial work with.

Sharon felt pretty confident about the informal assessment data. She and Trevor, another teacher in the school, administered the assessments, and they scored them together. They used authentic assessment tasks that had been circulated by the district, along with exemplars of student work and suggestions for instruction. The students actually read a range of materials and answered questions orally and in writing. After the class discussed the readings, the students wrote short essays based on the reading and the class discussion. The summary that she presented showed how many students they thought were in need of help. The English teachers used the information that the summary was based on to group students for instruction and to target their teaching strategies. In her view, this was excellent data that was not always used very well.

Although each school is a separate institution, each is part of a continuum of schooling for its students that encompasses all of the schools that the students have attended before and will attend later. Forging links between the various levels of schooling has always been a challenge. Sharing data can provide a powerful forum for discussion and shared decision making.

H. C. ANDERSEN STUDENTS IN SECONDARY SCHOOL

Dwayne didn't have any statistical data, but he had found out a lot from his meeting at the secondary school. He reported that the teachers there felt that students from H. C. Andersen did not have basic reading and writing skills and this lack jeopardized their success in their courses. In fact, the principal had given him a copy of a memo he had sent to H. C. Andersen's prior principal suggesting that they should meet to talk about how to prepare the students better for high school courses.

Dwayne's response to the "quality question" was straightforward. "They told me what they know, based on their experiences. They might be wrong but it's worth hearing."

Dwayne also mentioned that he was surprised that only a few of the students on his sports teams were on teams in high school. The competition was pretty high, so his stars did well, but most of the rest had chosen not to play on intramural teams. When his colleagues laughed at his research methods, he pointed out that he actually knew these kids and could do a "validity check" through personal observation.

On another note, Dwayne was impressed with the guidance teacher and her willingness to work closely with feeder schools. He thought they should nurture this relationship and maybe invite her to a team meeting at some point.

Data does not always come from within. It is also possible to refer to and draw on information from other jurisdictions and from national and even international resources to help frame, think about, and interpret evidence locally.

PROFESSIONAL RESOURCES

As the meeting ended, Janet mentioned that she had located a stack of articles about instruction and assessment for adolescent literacy. She handed out a list of titles and indicated that she thought these might be useful but they could wait until later. She would leave them with the librarian for checkout if anyone wanted them right away.

Assignment #10

A Quality Guide

If data are going to guide your thinking, you need to be sure that the data you are considering deserve your attention. Use Task Sheet #10 in the Resource section for each data source. Take a few minutes to go through this "quality exercise" so that you know how much you should rely on the data in your thinking. Ask yourself about reliability (confidence in the data), about validity (connection to what you want to understand), specificity (sufficiently detailed data), and limitations.

THE FIRST STROKES

The First Strokes

How do we make sense of this?

What does it all mean?

Once you have the data, the real fun begins. Educators are used to talking about their experiences. But they are not comfortable with using data to challenge their own and each other's ideas. They may even agree with Mark Twain's comment, "Lies, damn lies, and statistics." But statistics don't lie; people lie. And it is actually a good deal easier to lie without appealing to data and thinking about what it means than it is to manipulate data.

Data, by themselves, are benign. Meaning is brought to data through the human act of interpretation. Data are symbols that stand for sets of experiences. Making meaning from data is about using the symbols to reconstruct the underlying experiences. Engaging with data in this way is an active process. It requires taking an inquiry-minded approach to the data by asking questions such as, What do these data seem to tell us about our priority? What do they not tell us? What else would we need to know? And so on. Once meaning is brought to bear on the data through the interpretation process, it becomes possible to formulate messages to continue the conversations with key players.

When people use words to make false claims or offer unreasonable ideas, we don't blame the English language. Rather than trashing all statements with numbers in them, a more reasonable response is to learn enough about the statistics to distinguish honest, useful conclusions from skullduggery or foolishness.
—Abelson (1995)

Critical thinkers have the ability to identify the focus: the issue, question, or conclusion; analyze arguments; ask and answer questions of clarification and/or challenge; define terms, judge definitions, and deal with equivocation; identify unstated assumptions; judge the credibility of a source; observe, and judge observation reports; deduce, and judge deduction; induce, and judge induction; make and judge value judgments; consider and reason from premises, reasons, assumptions, positions, and other propositions with which they disagree or about which they are in doubt—without letting the disagreement or doubt interfere with their thinking ("suppositional thinking"); and, integrate the other abilities and dispositions in making and defending a decision.
—Ennis (1996)

Interpretation Is All

Even when there is broad consensus about the contents of some data source, the interpretation may be contested. Why? Because data do not answer questions. They provide lenses for analyzing working knowledge, observations, and professional judgments as you think about what the data mean for you.

Interpretation takes time and critical thought. As Ennis (1996) describes it, critical thinking "roughly means reasonable and reflective thinking focused on deciding what to believe and what to do" (page 1). He elaborates by identifying a series of dispositions and abilities that make up this complex constellation of activities. In his view, critical thinkers are disposed to care that their beliefs be *true* and that their decisions be justified; that is, care to "get it right" to the extent possible; care to present a position honestly and *clearly*, theirs as well as others; care about the *dignity* and *worth* of every person.

When you are considering data, it often helps to talk a little and then let the ideas "sit" for a bit. As Barth (2001) suggests, taking time to think will help to create meaningful change. And the best ideas come when people work together to share their ideas and try to make sense of the complexity. It is often difficult to take time to think in schools, but as we become more effective, reflective thinkers, we may make our schools not just different places but improved places for learning. Using data provides time for thinking, for reflecting, for new ideas, and for making meaning.

The full power of the inquiry process is unleashed when school staff work together, not in isolation, when data become a catalyst for constructive dialogue, and when school communities develop shared understandings and ownership of problems and solutions being pursued.
—Love (2000)

Sometimes this stage is frustrating and confusing. Scrutinizing data and looking for patterns and trends can lead to multiple interpretations and cause considerable consternation. Data may be contradictory; there will be anomalies; people will have different views of what is going on. And that is the reality of looking at data—not being sure, reserving judgment and considering all the possibilities, feeling confused and sometimes frustrated.

There is always the temptation to fall back to simpler interpretations, to dismiss new information, and avoid ideas that do not fit with past views—to paint a simpler, more familiar picture. But schools are vibrant, multifaceted, and contradictory places that deserve to be portrayed in all their complexity. And sometimes that means living with ambiguity.

Since the last meeting and the "unveiling of the data" there had been lots of discussion in the staff room at H. C. Andersen. The planning committee had taken all the "raw data" that they had collected so far and put it on the wall of the staff room, with their cautions about quality and the title:

"WHAT DOES IT ALL MEAN?????"

The planning committee asked the staff to spend time looking at the wall, jotting ideas on note paper, and sticking their ideas beside the data. They also started posting notices called "What the Data Say: Do You Agree?" beside the staff mailboxes, based on the ideas that were posted, with encouragement to the staff to add their comments to the wall.

Looking at data is time-consuming, but it can be fascinating. Different people will have different ideas, and the conversation will be wide-ranging. Interpretation takes discipline and hard work, so the process to consider it needs to be carefully planned to give people time and support to think about and challenge their views—individually and collectively. The hypotheses in educational planning are complex ones without simple answers, and there are (or should be) multiple data sets that need to be considered separately and in relation to one another. Facilitators for the process need to provide structure and direction while allowing freedom and encouraging the group to live with uncertainty while they investigate all of the data. And, at the end of the process, they may find that there are more questions rather than definitive answers. Why? Because education is complex, and it sometimes requires more time and attention to get clarity about all of the pertinent issues.

After a couple of weeks, the team extended an invitation to anyone on the H. C. Andersen staff who would be interested in being part of the "Interpretation Panel." They were going to have a "shortened day" of classes on December 8 and work from 2 until 7 (with dinner provided) to try to make sense out of the data.

Over half of the teachers signed up to come to the December 8 Interpretation Panel. A few asked Janet if they could use the time to finish their report cards, and the itinerant special education teacher wanted to work with a couple of teachers to develop IEPs for particular students for the next term. At first the support staff and custodians said that this was not really a necessary panel for them, but Janet suggested that she would love to have them there and valued their input, so some of them agreed.

At 2:00, teachers and support staff began arriving in the library for the meeting. They found the display from the staff room had been moved onto easels beside four round tables. Each of them was assigned to one of the tables so that the regular groups were mixed up. The planning group members were assigned to facilitate at tables—and they were not connected to the data that they felt the most strongly about. Janet had convinced them that they would get lots of chances to talk about their interpretations, but it was important to let the rest of the staff think about the data without being influenced by the experts. Instead, the group had created a set of generic questions, as well as particular processes for each of the data sources that the "interpretation groups" could use to consider the data and make sense of it. The generic questions were:

> • What is your initial interpretation of these data?
> • What patterns seem to be meaningful? Why?
> • What messages emerge from consideration of these data?
> • What is still confusing or not clear?

They had decided not to insist on any particular process for recording the ideas. Instead, each group could give their summary in any way that made sense to them. Group #1 would look at the State Assessment Data. Group #2 had three data sets—Attendance, Language in the Home, and the Community Survey. Group #3 was looking at the Informal Assessment of Reading and Writing. Group #4 was considering Success in Secondary School for H. C. Andersen students.

STATE LITERACY ASSESSMENT (GROUP #1)

Dwayne was leading the group that was considering the data from the state literacy test. He started by having them get clear about what the test measured and about what the table and graphs included. He also drew their attention to the cautions that Jason had identified. They were able to look at the scores by gender and grade, but Jason had not included data based on limited English proficient (LEP) students because some of the groups were so small that the statistics would be suspect. They did know that there was about a 5% difference in LEP students reaching the target for the district as a whole when they were compared with English first language students.

% of Students Reaching SAS (State Accountability Standard) in Reading and Writing				
	2003		2004	
Literacy (Grade 6)				
Reading	M	F	M	F
• State	78	83	79	83
• District	81	83	82	84
• H. C. Andersen	74 (139)	84 (128)	77 (132)	82 (127)
Writing	M	F	M	F
• State	75	77	77	78
• District	76	76	76	76
• H. C. Andersen	72 (139)	76 (129)	74 (130)	76 (127)
Literacy (Grade 7)				
Reading	M	F	M	F
• State	79	83	80	83
• District	81	84	82	83
• H. C. Andersen	77 (142)	80 (145)	75 (135)	82 (130)
Writing	M	F	M	F
• State	76	77	78	78
• District	77	77	77	76
• H. C. Andersen	80 (140)	79 (146)	73 (135)	75 (130)
Literacy (Grade 8)				
Reading	M	F	M	F
• State	81	83	80	82
• District	80	83	81	83
• H. C. Andersen	80 (160)	81 (144)	79 (136)	83 (133)
Writing	M	F	M	F
• State	77	77	81	83
• District	76	77	80	84
• H. C. Andersen	79 (179)	78 (144)	81 (136)	81(132)

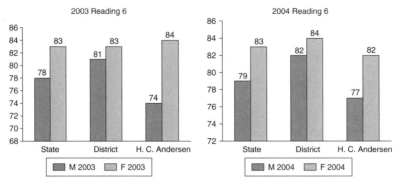

Percent of Students Reaching SAS in Reading by Gender 6th Grade: 2003 and 2004

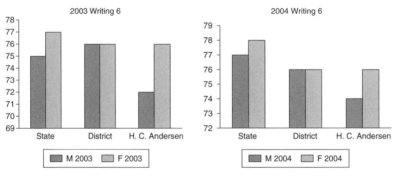

Percent of Students Reaching SAS in Writing by Gender 6th Grade: 2003 and 2004

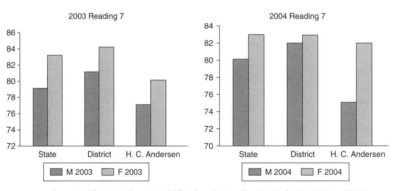

Percent of Students Reaching SAS in Reading by Gender 7th Grade: 2003 and 2004

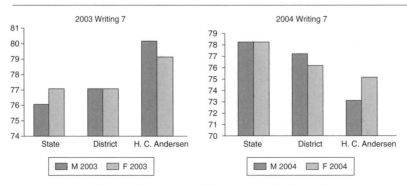

Percent of Students Reaching SAS in Writing by Gender 7th Grade: 2003 and 2004

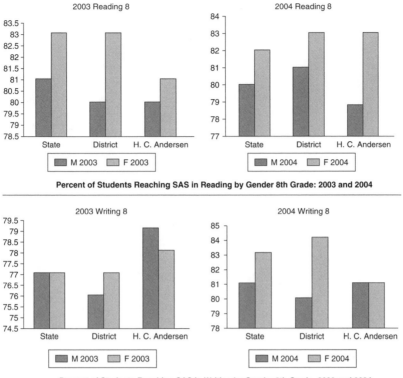

Percent of Students Reaching SAS in Reading by Gender 8th Grade: 2003 and 2004

Percent of Students Reaching SAS in Writing by Gender 8th Grade: 2003 and 2004

The conversation at Table 1 went like this:

I see three things that are interesting to me. One is we don't seem to be doing particularly well in relation to the state or in relation to the district in some instances . . . and we seem to be, in general, with a couple of exceptions . . . we seem to be in a state of decline. Although I realize two years isn't enough to say that. . . . Mind you that is also reflected in the state and the district as well, but that still shouldn't be an excuse for it, not addressing it.

There are two trends. There are some up trends, and there are some down trends, and I am trying to figure out if it is the reading or the writing that is actually the difference . . . 'cause if you look at 2003/ 2004 reading for eighth grade, our scores at least for the girls went up the next year, and then for the writing seven it went down. For writing eight it goes down. For reading seven it goes up. Did we shift our reading focus after we looked at the scores last year? Did we start . . . do you know what I am saying? Our reading scores for our females go up, and I am wondering if maybe we chose some books . . .

Yeah, but they only went up in eighth grade. In six they went down.

Another neat way of looking at it is. . . . I know our students tend to move around to a certain extent, but it might be interesting to kind of see what happens from our sixth grade to seventh, when we move from one year to the next. So if we take a look at our . . . take a look at our reading, our sixth-grade reading in 2003, and let's take a look at our seventh-grade reading in 2004. So you know what, they haven't actually changed a heck of a lot. It is pretty much the same group of students, well despite those who may have moved. So if we do the same thing . . . if we take a look at our seventh-grade reading in 2003 and then we take a look at our eighth-grade reading in 2004 . . . we haven't done very much. As a matter of fact we have gone down a little. The females have gone up a little bit, and the males have gone down a little bit. What about for the writing? If we do the sixth-grade writing . . . and then the seventh-grade writing . . . it is hard to tell. I never would have noticed our skills were different if you hadn't pointed that out.

These changes are pretty tiny—77 to 80% and then 79 to 80. You know what? We really aren't adding anything, it looks like. No. . . . so you know what? I won't be too quick to jump on the bandwagon that says things are in a huge decline if we actually take a look at the same group of kids moving through. But certainly it doesn't suggest that things are getting much better or that we are doing anything that is particularly effective.

The other thing is I am wondering about the test itself. Is it . . . do we feel it is reflective of our program?

Well, it sort of seems to me that if we take a look at the district as well . . . you know what? None of us are really doing very much. Nobody is really doing . . . everybody seems to be holding.

I don't agree. Writing in the state and the district actually went up fairly well where ours didn't from seventh grade to eighth grade.

Well, if you sort of look at the big picture, I don't think we are doing very well at all. We've got slightly under a quarter of our kids that are not meeting the standards and that seems to be not much better for the district and the state. Things don't really seem to be moving. If only 74% of our males are meeting the standard in literacy that is highly disturbing . . . a quarter of our school . . .

Maybe these are the students that we taught, but maybe they are the students that we haven't taught. We have to remember that we have a school with a transient population, a bunch of immigrant families. The new immigrants come to our school, and then they leave.

I know but I hate using that as an excuse, because I think that demographics get used far too often as an excuse for poor teaching. I think . . . my fear with our population changing is that more and more of our colleagues, not us of course, more and more of our colleagues tend to look at that and say, "What do you expect? These kids can't do much better; this is all we got to deal with." While I understand that that is a mediating factor, I would really hate for that to be used as an excuse for complacency.

Yup. I completely agree, but I think at the same time that this is why this is just one piece of information in one point and time. It is a little bit of a snap shot, but the snap shot is just . . . we could look at it one way and say, "Oh gosh, aren't we great! We are getting these high numbers with these immigrant students," but on the other hand we can say, "Wow, look at how many of them we're not exactly servicing very well."

What is kind of interesting about this is that we have this information, and if we were going to go back to our colleagues and talk about it, we could say that it seems like we are doing pretty well for a core group of students. We really need to address a couple of things: one, those students who are not obviously meeting the standard; and the other group are males.

It will be interesting when we talk to the other groups. Because I think that the group that is talking about the informal assessments for entering students might answer our question about how important this is.

So what do we know from this? We know that we have some males who are not doing very well, and our boys are consistently under district and state, with some anomaly with the seventh grade in 2003. Our females are, by and large, sort of holding their own.

You know what I want to know? Whether or not our special education students were included in this data or not. That may or may not make a difference to how I would understand that group of students that is not achieving the Accountability Standard.

I think that this is really good information to have, and it makes me feel incredibly concerned about the males.

Group #1 prepared their reporting chart to present to the whole staff, with answers to the questions that were posed initially.

Q.	What is your initial interpretation of these data?	A.	We are not sure. There are some trends, but they are not simple or straightforward.
Q.	What patterns seem to be meaningful? Why?	A.	There is a pattern for boys, which suggests we need to really find out what is going on with them. Mostly, boys are not doing as well as girls, except for one grade group.
			We are not doing well in relation to the district and the state, but we aren't sure if that is a problem or is this is what we should expect, given the students who come here.
Q.	What messages emerge from consideration of these data?	A.	We need to really focus on literacy for boys—at least to find out more about what the problem is.
Q.	What is still confusing or not clear?	A.	We want to have more information about the students who are in these classes and who was included in the test. We also need to find out what is actually tested on the state assessment.

ATTENDANCE, LANGUAGE IN THE HOME, AND COMMUNITY SURVEY (GROUP #2)

Sharon was facilitating the group that was assigned the attendance data, the census data about language in the home, and the community survey results. Right off the bat, the group wanted to draw relationships among them. Sharon, who was facilitating this group, cautioned them and quickly decided to have them consider each one in turn, as a separate issue. She reminded them that, within the attendance data, first they were looking at the average daily attendance for this school, with the same data for the district and the state, and then a graph of a snapshot averaged across a ten-week period at H. C. Andersen to give some detail.

Average Daily Attendance (% of enrollment): 2003–04			
	State	*District*	*H. C. Andersen*
6th grade - M	93.5	95.5	94.0
6th grade - F	93.0	96.0	95.0
7th grade - M	94.0	95.0	92.5
7th grade - F	94.0	95.5	95.0
8th grade - M	93.5	94.0	93.0
8th grade - F	94.0	95.0	94.0
Overall Average	93.6	95.1	93.9

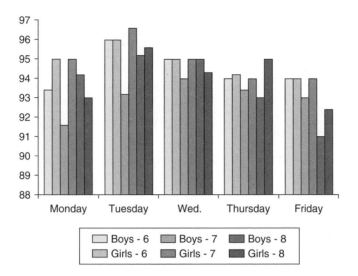

Here is the group's conversation:

> Well they are not coming in on Mondays . . . laughter . . . that must have been when we did the testing.
>
> The seventh-grade boys are consistently absent more than other groups, except eighth-grade boys on Friday; they don't seem to want to come as well.
>
> If I just take a look at the attendance, I don't actually see anything particularly disturbing other than the fact that we have Monday and Friday fall off, which doesn't really surprise me. We've got that little core group that maybe has to be looked at. I don't think that we are out of line. I don't see anything particular to us; we are slightly below the district with our attendance.
>
> It looks like we might want to think about some fun things to do on Friday afternoons . . . some whole school activities or something to encourage . . . You don't want this to become a trend. I would be curious to see what happens when they get to high school. Whether these trends actually hold or not.
>
> I would also like to know when . . . actually what 10-week period . . . when was this? 'Cause if they did this in December or . . . or around Thanksgiving . . . I would like to think they wouldn't have done it in December . . . or any other significant time.
>
> But, would that make a difference for boys and girls?
>
> We need to ask the planning committee about this.

Okay, that would be good. It is not that you want to excuse absenteeism; I know that it is important, but we need to know what we can assume from this data.

But why are they not coming to school? Who is not coming to school? Because if our students are doing fine, and they are not coming to school because they are bored, or they don't come to school on Friday and still do just fine, then we may just have to challenge them. But if it is the kids that are not doing well, then it may be the same kids that don't pass our standards test. We need to know that.

The other thing that would be helpful, as you said, is who is not coming, and what percentage of these is chronic? Chronic offenders or chronically ill?

No. Exactly. Maybe we could do Friday lunch hour things.

We don't really know why they aren't attending.

Yeh, if we found out that many of our students were not attending because of work. Many of those were absent for reasons of helping out at home or helping out with childcare . . . then maybe there is some good information to know.

So it would be good to know why they are away. We have some good information, but we need lots more. This in itself does not really tell me anything. It just creates more questions for me. Which are good questions actually . . . it would be really good to know why this is actually all going on. Right off the bat I would say we have to do some more things on Fridays.

I also think that seventh-grade boys group, we need to do something; we need to find out why they are not coming to school. If we can do something to target them then maybe the eighth-grade group will start coming when they reach the next year. We are still capturing most of our kids. It is just that small percentage that is not coming in. It is the same in the state and in the district.

Well, it is. You are bound to have a certain percentage who are actually sick on any one day and actually shouldn't be there. I want to know how many of these kids we should be concerned about.

Jason said he used our attendance records. I'll bet he could do more analysis for us.

We'd better be sure that the records are good then.

Then the group addressed the data about language of home from the census:

% of Homes Where English is Not the First Language: 2001	
State	42%
District	40%
H. C. Andersen	43%

Here is what they had to say:

> I don't really know what to make of this stuff. It's four years old. It looks like we are pretty similar to the district and the state. I don't think that is true. We are an immigrant school.
>
> I think one of the things that I would like to see is to have another little survey to get this. We need current information about language in the home for our school. So maybe that is what we would like . . . some current data because we don't know really much about this. Again because we have a transient population so we don't know whether the census is accurate any more.

Finally, the group looked at the needs identified by community members from the Community Survey:

- Education: Adult and youth computer training, better schools, tutorial program, and library access
- Community Activities: Afterschool programs, parks, and expanded Boys & Girls Club activities
- Affordable Child Care: Sick and well
- English as a Second Language classes for adults
- Transportation
- Healthcare (affordable)
- Teen Programs (At-Risk Youth)
- Neighborhood Clean-up/Beautification

Here is their discussion:

> I love their concern about better schools. I would love to know what that means. Adult and youth computer training, I understand that, tutorial library access, but better schools. . . . I would like to know what "better" means. Does better mean schools where they feel more comfortable coming in and more open? Or does it mean that we think that our programming is not up to the standard? That would be really helpful for me.
>
> Take a look at the needs identified by the community members. They have identified learning a new language as something as well. We could build on that.

I wonder if the community activities that we run actually help capture some of those kids that don't like to come to school. We probably don't run them on Fridays.

It looks like they are asking for a teen program for at-risk youth. I would like to know what they want. Does that have to do with having activities or some sort of support network? Do we want to partner them up with a high school?

Group #2 spent a fair bit of time preparing their report. They wanted to communicate two messages. First, they really felt that they needed to know more to use the information that they were considering; and second, they realized that they needed to make connections among the different pieces of data, and they probably also needed to see what the others were looking at as well. Here is their graphic presentation of their discussion.

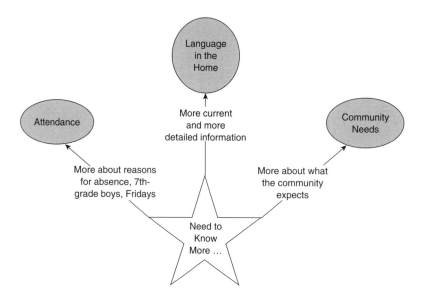

INFORMAL ASSESSMENT OF
READING AND WRITING (GROUP #3)

The group that was looking at the informal assessments was buzzing right from the beginning. Sharon had really wanted to lead this table but she was pretty happy that her colleague Trevor was there. He had worked with her to do the assessments and certainly understood them. Sharon had created a simple process for the group to look at the data, and Sylvia was facilitating the group.

Working together, they first looked at the assessment that Sharon and Trevor used and talked about what it was measuring and what they might learn from it.

	# of 6th-Grade Students Struggling With . . .			
	2000–01 322 students	2001–02 304 students	2002–03 275 students	2003–04 256 students
Reading				
text structure	22	25	34	21
syntax and grammar	50	52	42	7
orthographic knowledge (word patterns)	25	26	26	20
comprehension (inference, summarizing, testing assumptions, organizing)	255	267	240	217
Writing				
voice (personal style)	150	139	122	110
organization (logical plan and sequence)	260	255	234	189
ideas and content (purpose, focus, and supporting ideas)	221	237	216	190
conventions	175	162	155	136
use of language (fluency, use of figurative language)	244	196	160	142

Sylvia told them that the numbers were actual numbers of students that Trevor and Sharon felt were struggling with reading and writing when they arrived at H. C. Andersen from the reading and writing assessments that they did using authentic assessment tasks that have been circulated by the district.

The conversation within the group went like this:

When I first saw this I said: Oh my god. They don't understand anything they are reading. Wow, that is fascinating. But phonetically we are teaching them very well.

Well, actually it is the elementary school.

Oh good, we can blame them.

You know, it would have been so helpful if we knew which of these students were identified as having learning needs anyway . . . and which of these students are LEP. I mean, there is no way to understand this comprehension number . . .

Just the fact that we have . . . so many . . . almost two-thirds of these students having problems with comprehension. I cannot believe that that is not related to something else that is going on. Mind you, it is interesting when you take a look at their organization and writing. It is disturbing as well.

I was looking at their writing. It is not surprising that they can't write either, because if they can't understand what they are reading then it is not really shocking that they are not able to organize their own work and their own ideas to communicate it in writing . . . and use the language.

Well, I don't quite know how to really understand all of this except to say we have a big problem with writing . . . massive problems with writing. Particularly with organization. Obviously something is happening . . . it seems to get better . . . a little bit but not really . . .

The numbers are way down, but the percentage of students that are having a problem are probably not that different. We have a declining enrollment, remember.

Okay, so we have to keep that in mind.

I don't even know what to make of this because I don't know who these students are. I know nothing else about them, and I am hesitant to start saying anything.

We definitely know that in reading we have a comprehension problem . . . that we can say. That should be maybe a target of focus in sixth grade . . . but the other thing is this is information that we might want to hand back to the elementary school . . .

Of course they may know this already.

So, obviously we have a real problem with comprehension. It would be good for the teachers to know that when they are taking a look at their reading programs, they are really going to have to focus heavily on the tasks around comprehension.

We don't even teach reading here. Maybe the English teachers do some, but I don't in science and geography. I just assume they can read.

I wonder how many of these kids come from families where they don't speak English?

Whatever, the fact is we have a really big problem with comprehension and we still have to focus on that, no matter what the reason is. Obviously, in writing we have lots of problems around ideas and organization. That is really good information to know. We need to think about how to make it fit our programs.

Do you know what else I think would be useful . . . is if we did this in sixth grade and we did it again in eighth grade. . . . Then this would give us some information about how much the kids have learned over their time here.

Do we really want that information? (laughter)

Yes we do. We need that information; it is a good piece of information.

We need to bite the bullet and find out how much we have taught them. I bet we're pleasantly surprised.

I need the other side . . . and I think that the sixth-grade teachers need to come together and look at this and figure out where they want to prioritize and how to organize programs right now.

Not just the sixth grade. All the grades.

I don't really feel comfortable saying that two-thirds . . . well, yes, two-thirds of the students are having problems with comprehension, for example . . . and actually more than that when we take a look at 2003/2004 . . . virtually all of them . . .

For me as a teacher using this information and understanding it . . . I need to know who these students are, why they are having problems with comprehension. That would help me decide how I am going to program and what strategies I might use for working with them.

It would also help to know who are the students that get it . . . then why are they able to get it . . . because they are a smaller percentage.

But, if 217 out of 256 are having problems with comprehension and there are also high numbers with organization and ideas, contents and writing . . . this is a lot . . . this is actually really disturbing.

It would be good to know . . . . I would really love to know as well what program . . . how many of these kids are coming straight from our feeder schools and have been in the district from kindergarten and have moved up through.

I don't think we have records that would give us that. Maybe we would have to start keeping better track.

The other thing I am wondering is the male/female ratio. I would like to know if we have a difference in where the males are having difficulties and where the females are having difficulties, because we could probably target instruction . . . we would choose readings differently.

> You know if virtually all of our sixth graders are having problems with comprehension, I would be curious to know how they are doing on their state tests. We need to bring this up with the whole group.
>
> When it came to the key messages that emerged from the data, this group focused on trying to write a simple, clear statement of their interpretations. This proved to be more difficult than they thought it would be. They found that they had many more questions than before. And they were perplexed.

New Learning

There are students at H. C. Andersen who need support becoming good readers. A small number need intensive attention to acquire the skills of decoding and language structure. Many need support in the area of comprehension (inference, summarizing, testing assumptions, organizing).

Writing is a significant problem for at least half of the students in the school, in all areas—voice, organization, ideas and content, conventions, and use of language. We have particular concern about ideas and content and organization.

Perplexing Questions

There is so much we don't know.

How does this information relate to the state assessment scores? Which one is right?

Who are the students and what else do we know about them? Can we find out more?

What does this information mean for the way we teach and the programs that we offer?

SUCCESS IN SECONDARY SCHOOL (GROUP #4)

The group who were considering H. C. Andersen students' success in the secondary school was joined by the guidance counselor, the English head, the coach, and the LEP teacher from Strathmere. Janet was leading this group. There really wasn't much formal data, except for this letter to the prior principal.

Dec. 15, 2003

Strathmere High School

Dear Mr. ████ ,

It was interesting talking to you at the meeting last week. As we discussed, this letter is a formal statement of some of the trends that we are observing at Strathmere. We have been looking at the student success rate in ninth-grade classes in relation to their feeder schools. The students who come to us from H. C. Andersen seem to be having difficulty in some of their academic classes. Although it is only the end of the first term, a number of students from Andersen are at risk of failure in several courses, especially science and English. The relevant members of my staff and I would be very willing to meet with you and some of your teachers to discuss this matter and perhaps frame some interventions to improve the students' transition to secondary schools.

Your sincerely,
Principal

Janet took this opportunity to have the staff from H. C. Andersen learn from their secondary colleagues. She had asked the group to come to the session with questions that they wanted to explore. After initial introductions the conversation began.

Strathmere guidance counselor: I can't tell you how excited we are to be here for this meeting. We've never been invited to attend planning sessions before, and we really want to make the transition to Strathmere as good as it can be for your kids.

Janet: We're excited too. We hope that you can help us understand what happens to our students when they get to you. Dwayne was pretty impressed with what you are doing, but he was surprised at how little we really know about one another's world.

HCA teacher: We were also embarrassed by the letter that your principal had sent. No one here even knew about it.

Strathmere coach: Never mind, moving forward is more important. So, do you have specific questions for us?

Janet: It seems to me that we might spend some time making a concept map of the questions that we have. I'll write the ideas as the group from here call them out.

HCA teacher: Well, we're really grappling with how little we know about how our students do when they leave us. We thought things were okay, but now it looks like maybe some of them have trouble academically, and they don't really even excel in sports as a substitute. We want to know how they are doing in class but out of class too. How are they fitting in? What is their social life like?

HCA teacher: The letter says that some of them are having trouble with English and with science? Is this different from other feeder schools? Do all feeder schools get a letter like this? Or is it just us? How do you know they are having trouble? What evidence do you use?

HCA teacher: What kinds of trouble are our kids having? Why aren't they succeeding? Are they attending school? Are there particular categories of students who are having difficulty—girls, boys, athletes, LEP, whatever?

HCA teacher: What interventions are in place at Strathmere? What support can our students get when they move to secondary school?

HCA teacher: No matter what you do, it is a big kick in the side of the head for these kids to move from eighth grade to ninth grade anyway. Even when they are strong students it is stressful. It would be great to know what you at the high school feel middle schools should do, because we are obviously not doing something very well and it is disturbing.

After a while the concept map began to take form.

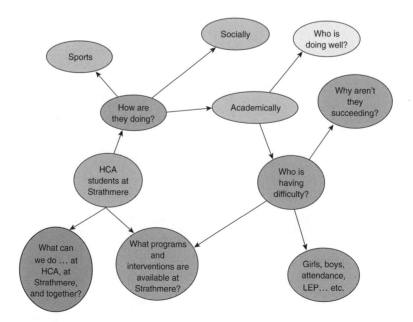

Now it was time for the Strathmere group to jump in.

Guidance counselor: Wow, lots of questions. Let me start by saying that you have covered all of the issues that we talked about before we came here today, and then some. I'll start trying to answer some of them. First of all, our principal sent that letter last year, after a conversation with your former principal. None of the other feeder schools received one. That doesn't mean that we don't have concerns about students from other schools as well, but we were noticing some patterns with kids from here. We were hoping to start some kind of transition team with members from both schools to figure out what was going on. So, we don't really have all the answers. We have a bunch of questions as well.

English head: When students come to Strathmere, we do a short informal literacy assessment with them so we can place them in the right English courses. One of the things that we noticed was that quite a few students from H. C. Andersen were uncomfortable with writing, and the short essays that we had them write were disorganized and not very sophisticated. They weren't horrible, but their writing was pretty childish, and they didn't seem to have a feel for how to turn thoughts into written work for an outside audience. In class, they seemed to get the ideas and could talk about them pretty well. But their ideas lost their power when they had to write them. When we gave them a multiple choice reading assessment, most did fine on the structure and grammar segments, but a lot of them had trouble with comprehension, especially if it involved inference or problem solving. That's what we had hoped to talk to you about when the letter was sent.

Coach: You mentioned sports. I know H. C. Andersen has a strong athletic program that involves many students in competitions outside the school. We have lots of teams as well, but most of them are intramural and are designed to give students a chance to participate in physical activity and acquire a taste for sport as a life-long activity. We do have some varsity teams, but mostly we focus on sports that they will be able to do long after they leave school—sports like tennis, volleyball, soccer, golf, and martial arts. And we also encourage all students to match an athletic extracurricular activity with another one like dance, drama, debating, chess, or fashion design. We think it gives them many more options. I've noticed that H. C. Andersen students don't get as involved as we expected, given their background with athletics here. I wonder if the students who come to us from H. C. Andersen think intramurals are low status. And maybe they find that they have limited exposure to these other things and tend to shy away from them. I don't know. It's just a thought.

Guidance counselor: On the social side, I would say that your students generally fit in very well, once they get settled, especially in ninth grade. But I have been seeing some of the tenth graders recently who are trying to decide what courses to take next year, and they seem to be losing their confidence. I think it has to do with not being sure that they have the skills that they need to take the courses that would prepare them to go to college. Mr. Balacco isn't here but he teaches science and math, and he wanted me to mention that he works a lot with H. C. Andersen students to make sure that they have the basics that they need to do the more complex work in his classes.

LEP teacher: You also asked if there were particular groups of students who are having trouble. I think we would agree that boys have more trouble academically and socially. This is not just boys from H. C. Andersen. We see it generally. We track attendance patterns as well and find that boys are also more likely to skip school. This is a top priority for us this year—staying on top of who is absent and why. And intervening early. We also keep a close eye on our LEP students. We have them "buddied" with other students in their classes who help them when the language gets in the way, as well as taking an LEP course each semester. And, you know, they seem to be holding their own pretty well. I am delighted by how well they are doing.

The group was surprised that their time was finished. Janet asked each of the Strathmere teachers if they would be willing to report their responses to the whole group, based on the notes that she had taken. Here is a summary of what they felt they had learned about H. C. Andersen students when they went to Strathmere:

- Many have trouble with writing (especially organization and expressing complex ideas).
- Few get involved in extracurricular activities (not even intramural sports).
- Most fit in well socially.
- Some lack academic confidence.
- Boys adjust less well than girls (academically and socially, also more absences).
- LEP students are doing pretty well.

Janet invited everyone to move to the staff room where they were assigned seats to mix up the groups over dinner. It was a very talkative but contemplative group that sat down to digest ideas, along with their food.

Considering the data and arriving at group interpretations is a challenging and rewarding task that often leaves the participants feeling as if they finally have the answers that they need, and they are ready to move on. This is a crucial juncture because they have not all had the same experience, and there are many others who need to learn from their work without having to go through the complete process personally. Somehow the group has to capture what has happened and emerged from the data as a starting point for sharing what they have learned.

After dinner, everyone returned to the meeting room to hear the results from each of the groups. Thomas, realizing that it was getting late and people were getting tired, suggested that they hear from each group and have discussion only for clarification at this point and let the planning committee consolidate the issues and bring their summary back to the staff at the next meeting. He also suggested that someone from Strathmere might want to join the planning committee, at least for the next few meetings. They agreed to send a representative. As they reported, Janet took notes so that she could create a concept map of the ideas to share with the whole staff. Here is the beginning concept map that she created from the various presentations.

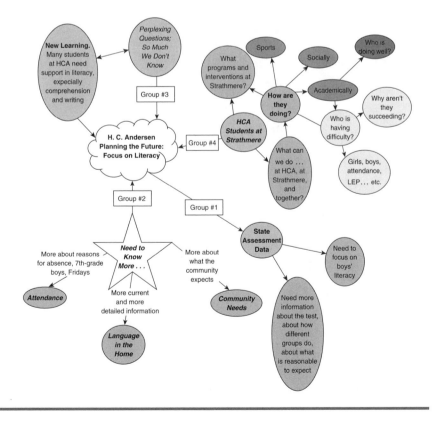

Assignment #11

A Guide to Interpretation

Once you have multiple data sources available, the real work begins—making sense of it all. You need to organize a process for members of the team to have time together for engagement with and discussion about what the data mean. You need an interpretation session just to get familiar with what is there, in the individual data sources first.

Using Task Sheet #11 in the Resource section, have a small group consider *each data source* and think about what it might mean. What patterns do you see? Share your ideas with each other.

Have someone make notes about all of the possible interpretations. If someone disagrees with an idea, mark it with an asterisk and carry on with other interpretations.

Highlight anything that is confusing or not clear.

Note anything that might change the interpretation.

Debrief the discussions from each group and *compile all of the interpretations from all of the data sources* together in a concept map and see what emerges.

Creating a
Culture of Inquiry

Making sense of the data is a challenging activity, but it is only the first step. As we see it, the ultimate success of considering different data sources with different uses will be the establishment of a culture of inquiry—schools that are not only engaged in looking at data to understand themselves better but that act on their learning to change what they do and are willing to share what they learn with others. This is not a static process. It is a way of thinking and of interacting that goes beyond periodic meetings and becomes part of the cultural glue that holds a school together. Data form the foundation for faculty to inquire together into the relationships between their practices and student learning as they continually grow and refine their professional expertise and practice.

THE IMAGE GROWS

Considering data does not produce obvious answers. In fact, teams often find that they have more questions, and they get drawn into a search for more information.

> **The Image Grows**
>
> What does this picture include?
>
> What will we do as a result of our new knowledge?

Consensus About the Interpretation

One of the first things that teams discover when they begin to work with a range of data is that different sources of data may lead to different conclusions. There are rarely obvious and dramatic findings. Instead, a composite picture emerges as they talk about and think about what the data may represent. One of the first tests that researchers use in considering data is the "reasonableness test": Does this make sense? Sometimes the discussion can be heated and emotional as people find that some of their beliefs and convictions do not hold up in relation to the evidence. As they engage in the discussion about how the various interpretations support and challenge their hypotheses, the team needs to be sensitive to how the new information will be received by individuals on the team. The trick is to examine and question ideas without challenging the worth of the people who hold them and to routinely ask themselves about how it all fits together. Over time, they can move towards tentative conclusions and make decisions about what actions to take, with some confidence that they can focus their work and justify their choices with evidence.

They also become very aware of the many things that they do not know much about that could influence their plans. So they move forward with purpose, but with humility, caution, and a willingness to reconsider their plans as they learn more. Once again, this is an iterative process that requires some mechanism for integrating information into a workable image. Teams should also expect that there will be differences of opinion that will require more discussion and often more data.

After the meeting of interpretation teams, the planning committee met to compile all of the interpretations and formulate some recommendations for action. Each of them arrived with their boxes and bags of materials from the tables that they facilitated, and notebooks full of their own reflections and notes. They realized very quickly that they were still a long way away from having a coherent picture of the school. But they did know a lot more than they might have predicted when they began this process. Now they had to try to pull everything together and recommend some directions for action. Thomas suggested that they start the discussion by going back to the questions and hypotheses that they had generated at their earlier meeting to see what they had learned.

Preliminary Questions	Hypotheses	Insights From the Data
Which students are doing well in relation to literacy, and which ones are having difficulty?	There is a group of young boys who are having problems.	Mostly boys are not doing as well as girls, and there is a particular identifiable group of boys (now in seventh grade) who are disengaged, skip school, and are not learning to read and write.

Preliminary Questions	Hypotheses	Insights From the Data
Are there differences in literacy related to student, family and school characteristics, specifically gender, attendance, participation in sports, family circumstances, educational history, grade, and homework?	Students who come from "new" populations are less familiar with English and have trouble with language skills.	We don't know the language background of students who are struggling with reading and writing, but LEP makes a difference in the district, so it is likely that we have some LEP students who need focused attention.
		Almost half of the students (boys and girls) are not competent in writing, in all grades.
		We have individual diagnostic information about every student in sixth grade this year and who was in sixth grade last year. This gives us a lot of information that we can use to identify individual students and groups of students who need specific instruction and/or practice in reading and writing.
	Students would do better if parents helped them with homework.	It looks like there is a lot we can do in the school without depending on parents to help, but perhaps we can provide parents with tasks that they can do with their children that will be directly connected to what we are trying to do at school.
What kinds of literacy problems are the students having?	Students at H. C. Andersen might have identifiable patterns of confusion or difficulty in literacy that could be targeted for remediation.	A small number of students need intensive instruction to acquire the skills of decoding and language structure; many need support in reading comprehension, and at least half need teaching, practice, and feedback to improve their writing.

(Continued)

Preliminary Questions	Hypotheses	Insights From the Data
	Students from H. C. Andersen do fine when they get to high school.	H. C. Andersen students actually struggle when they get to high school. They fit in pretty well, but they are not really engaged in school activities, and their academic skills (especially in writing and comprehension) are weak.
What literacy teaching and assessment strategies appear to be most effective with middle school kids?	A schoolwide focus on literacy would enhance reading and writing.	There is a need for a schoolwide focus on literacy.

During the interpretation process, some issues become quite clear, while others remain murky. This is the time to decide which ones you feel confident about and agree about, which ones deserve immediate attention, and which ones you need to know more about.

Reviewing their initial hypotheses gave the H. C. Andersen team a beginning picture, but as Dwayne commented, "We learned a lot more than this at our interpretation meeting."

The committee started to sift through all of the material from the interpretation groups. When the discussion was getting a little chaotic, Thomas decided that they should use index cards to write down ideas and put their new learning into three categories—things we are now pretty sure about and need to act on, things we think are important insights that deserve attention, and things we need to know more about. Everyone took a stack of index cards and wrote their ideas on the cards. When they were finished they posted them on the wall under the headings. The discussions were aimed at getting some consensus. When they all stood back and looked at the statements, it was clear that they had identified many of the same issues, but there was not a lot of agreement about what should go in each category.

They all agreed that they needed to do something about the seventh-grade boys, although some felt that they didn't know enough yet to move forward with a plan.

There was consensus that literacy had to be an immediate focus but disagreement about the grades that needed attention and whether they should focus on reading or writing or both.

Dwayne was still not convinced that the school wasn't much more diverse than the district, although Jason was able to explain that there were some schools that were much more diverse in the inner city and that affected the average for the district. In fact, H. C. Andersen did serve a very diverse population with many different languages and cultures.

There was lots of concern about how the students fared at Strathmere. Sharon was sure that the literacy focus would change things. Sylvia thought the school should really focus on a transition strategy with the secondary school. The coach from Strathmere (who had joined the group) agreed and suggested that perhaps H. C. Andersen needed to rethink its extracurricular program as well as the academic one.

Janet knew that she wanted to put an immediate plan in place, but she was pretty astonished not only by the limited agreement but also by how much they didn't know. When they took a stretch break, she talked to Thomas, and they decided to push ahead towards some decisions, at least about the key issues that they should act on.

After the break, Thomas asked the group to vote about the things that required immediate action and categorize the other issues into the other categories (for now). Here is the chart that emerged:

WHAT WE AGREE ABOUT!!!

Things We Are Sure About And Need to Act On

There is a group of boys (now in seventh grade) who need immediate and thoughtful attention to capture their interest, build their confidence, and ensure that they develop literacy skills.

Kids can't learn if they aren't in school, and we have quite a few unexplained absences (as well as some concern about how accurate the attendance data might be).

Many of our students do not have the kind of skills in reading that they need to succeed academically, especially the higher order skills that are necessary to read and understand complex text.

Writing is a significant problem for at least half of our students.

Important Insights That Deserve Attention

Our students are not well prepared for secondary school, socially or academically.

The community is concerned about having good schools.

Staff at the school is going to change in the next few years because of retirements, and we are going to lose expertise.

The school's athletic program is good, but it may not be all that we need.

Areas We Need to Know More About

Our student body is diverse, but we need to know more about the nature of the diversity and how it might influence what we do.

Some kids appear not to be interested and engaged in school, and we need to find out who they are, why they aren't engaged, and what we can do we do about it.

We need to know a lot about what kind of programs our kids need to become good at reading and writing.

We would like to know more about how to establish better connections with the parents and the community.

This session was exhausting. None of the planning team had expected that it would be so hard to agree about the interpretations so that they could move forward with a set of shared goals and an agreed upon action plan. As Sylvia said, "I always thought everyone agreed with my ideas. Now I see that there are lots of different ways of thinking about things. Some of the things that we've talked about have never occurred to me before." There were lots of nods around the room.

Thomas suggested that they take some time to reflect on their discussions and reconvene the next day to formulate some short- and medium-term plans that they could take to the whole staff.

Assignment #12

Consensus About Interpretations

Working with data does not produce obvious answers out of the fog. Instead it brings issues and ideas to the surface for discussion and clarification. This can be a difficult time because you are so close to making decisions, and you will discover that you have a range of points of view to reconcile. It requires patience, sensitivity, and trust.

Use Task Sheet #12 in the Resource section and begin by having each member write single ideas on index cards and post them under these three headings:

- Things We Are Sure About And Need to Act On
- Important Insights That Deserve Attention
- Areas We Need To Know More About

Have a discussion about what statements actually belong under the headings and why, always listening to the ideas of others and trying to understand their point of view.

Prepare a chart of your decisions.

Moving to Action

Once you have a shared image of the issues, planning solutions is the fun part. Educators are generally action-oriented, and this is the time for action. With a place to start and everyone heading in the same direction with the same vision, you can think about programs, map interventions, locate resources, decide what professional development you need, and on and on. This does not mean that the actions should be planned in haste or depend on someone's favorite approach. But at this stage, educators find themselves in the realm of the familiar—a place where they have lots of experience. At the same time, it is useful to have a process for connecting people to actions.

By the next day, the group was more animated, and it was clear that they had been thinking about their task. Dwayne and Sylvia had talked on the phone the previous evening and asked it they could present a skeleton plan to the group as a starting point. Everyone agreed that it would be good to have something to work from.

Sylvia began by saying that she and Dwayne really thought that the work they had done should be shared with the staff and that the whole staff needed to be involved in the detailed action planning.

They were also concerned that there had to be connections among the various plans so that the coherence that had been achieved didn't get lost in translation. As Dwayne said, "If we're going to completely revamp the extracurricular program, I want it to really help our kids, not just be different than it is now." He suggested that the planning committee would still have to be the clearing house and make the links.

The organizer that they presented was designed using the work from the prior day as scaffolding for the whole staff to move to action. First, they had turned the consensus statements into action statements, but it was pretty clear that there was still a lot of work to be done for these statements to become a reality in the school. So they had added columns for the staff to choose where they wanted to be involved.

Category	Actions	Team Leader	Team Members
Plan for Immediate Action	Intensive interventions for 7th-grade boys		
	Tracking absences through accurate and current data and intervening immediately		
	Schoolwide literacy initiative with a focus on comprehension in reading and on writing		

(Continued)

Category	Actions	Team Leader	Team Members
Plan for Next Year	Revamp of extracurricular program		
	Transition program from H. C. Andersen to Strathmere		
	Identify staff requirements and skill sets for the next few years		
Investigate and Report	Detailed description of the student body		
	Systematic identification of students who are potentially at-risk		
	Programs for enhancing adolescent literacy		
	Range of professional development activities for adolescent literacy		
	Strategies for establishing better connections with parents and the community		

Dwayne finished the presentation by saying, "Sorry for being so directive here, but we think this has been an amazing experience, and we don't want to lose the momentum. But if the staff isn't all on board, nothing will really happen. We need everyone pulling in the same direction." He actually blushed when he added, "Oh yeah, there is one more action that I think this planning committee has to take responsibility for. We have to identify the indicator categories and data that we need to monitor our progress along the way."

The other members of the planning committee weren't sure what to say. Then Thomas stood up, shook both their hands, and said, "I think you two have captured the essence of the next stage of the process. And I very much agree that we have to involve everyone now."

Janet knew that Dwayne and Sylvia's plan was a good one and they would be effusive advocates for it. But she also knew that their excitement would alienate some of the staff, and she was pretty confident that they would agree. She suggested that the next step was to involve the whole staff in an exercise with the concept map to show how it had developed from the interpretation panel's work and how it linked to the organizer for action. The rest of the meeting was spent planning on working with the material at the next staff meeting.

Even though planning teams have been intimately involved, agreement about directions and ownership of ideas are essential if the whole school is going to embark on any new initiatives, or if the school is going to give up some longstanding activities. Do not expect that your enthusiasm and new knowledge will travel by osmosis. Everyone has to have a chance to make the plan their own.

The first part of the next staff meeting was dedicated to reviewing the concept map and the "What We Agree About!" chart. The team had invited members of each of the interpretation groups (not the planning team members) to describe the process and their discussions and to make their presentation to the whole staff. Then they broke into groups, and the team members facilitated discussions for clarification. After a ten-minute discussion, Janet put out some sheets of colored dots. Everyone was asked to put a green dot on ideas in the "What We Agree About!" chart on the statements that they also agreed about, a yellow dot if they were unsure about the statement, and a red dot if they did not agree. Anyone who put a yellow or a red dot on a statement was given a chance to ask questions or explain their thinking. Janet was relieved that there were very few yellow dots and only one red one (on establishing better relationships with the community).

To close the meeting, she told them that Dwayne and Sylvia had taken the material and created a tentative action chart that would be posted in the staff room. Janet asked everyone to have a look, think about where they would like to work, and sign up, sometime during the next week, for at least one of the teams. She had already approached staff members to lead the teams. Trevor had agreed to lead the intervention team for seventh-grade boys. Tracking absences went to the VP (Drew), as long as Jason was willing to help him. Sharon was the obvious choice for the literacy initiative. Dwayne and Sylvia asked if they could work on the Transition Program and the revamp of extracurricular programs together and involve the guidance counselor and the coach from Strathmere. Janet figured that she had better look at the staffing issues herself. The actions that required investigation and reporting she left without leaders for the time being. At the meeting she suggested these might be areas that some of the rest of the staff might take on as short-term research projects. And they did. There was a good deal of milling around and silliness as staff members signed up for the teams that they wanted to join. Janet was pleased with their attitude and apparent willingness to be involved.

Once the teams were formed, Janet suggested that the team leaders might come to the next school council meeting to present the process and progress to date, and maybe even invite members of the school council to join teams if they were interested. She also announced the end of the ad hoc planning committee and invited anyone on staff to volunteer to form the School Improvement Team that would replace it. And she asked Thomas to continue as chair. They would determine a process for selection after they knew who was interested.

The School Improvement Team scheduled a meeting in two weeks to review progress and set a schedule for the year.

Assignment #13

Moving to Action

Although it is the stage that feels familiar, moving to action is where the work flourishes or fades. Everyone has to at least support the vision that has emerged, and most people have to be willing to participate. Deciding what to do and who will do it cannot be left to chance.

You need a detailed plan for each of the action statements that you have identified. Use Task Sheet #13 in the Resource section to guide your thinking.

Start by finding someone (or ones) who will provide leadership for each team.

Put a structure in place that gives teams some direction to begin their work, let them know what they are expected to do and by when, and give them time and support to carry on.

Bring key players together regularly to check progress, maintain coherence, identify problems, brainstorm solutions, and think about what you will accept as evidence that your work is having the desired effect.

DISPLAYING THE PICTURE

Once schools get involved in using data, they may forget that they are not the only ones who are interested in what they are learning. At this stage in the process you need to think carefully about what insights and ideas are emerging from consideration of the data, who is interested, how to deliver the key messages to the various audience(s), and how to continue the accountability *conversations* so that a broad range of people can respond and be part of formulating plans for action.

> **Displaying the Picture**
>
> How will we engage the audience?
>
> How will we share what we have learned?

If professional accountability is characterized by ongoing conversations, these conversations should be regular, recurring opportunities for an evolutionary understanding of student learning, and of student, parent, and teacher aspirations for the student. Professional accountability as conversation means broadening the range of contact and the content under discussion.

Traditionally, there are few structures and traditions for teachers to come together with the community to discuss problems or celebrate successes. Isolation is the institutionalized norm (Mitchell & Sackney, 2000).

This culture of privacy is accompanied by a general fear of exposure and a reluctance to share. But there are many reasons why schools and their communities should work together for the sake of the students. Routine sharing can ensure that the conversations are not focused on only a few messages or responding to concerns.

In our view, one time to engage in conversations that go beyond the issue at hand is when large-scale test results are released. The fact that there is always consternation when test results are reported suggests to us that most schools lack a genuine culture of inquiry. The first response is usually one of pride and acceptance of accolades (from schools on the top of the charts) and excuses (from schools near the bottom). This kind of reactive response not only gives one data source considerably more credibility than it deserves, it also ignores all of the other things that are related to achievement and that are priorities for schools. As we see it, this occasion provides an ideal opportunity for schools to position the annual release of central test data as one small piece of information that they need to incorporate into an already complex series of data pictures that they are routinely developing to show where they have been and where they are now and that offer some images of the future as well. It is a chance to situate the large-scale assessments in a context of shared values and develop a shared vision for the school.

Engaging the Audiences

So how do you go about engaging the various audiences in conversations about data? Earlier in the book we suggested that you identify the range of audiences who are likely to be interested in learning more about the school. You may have identified other staff members, students, parents, or community groups. But it is not enough to summarize your data and present it to the various audiences. Accountability as conversation is part of an ongoing process of engagement and interaction that is rooted in trust and a willingness to be open to ideas and debate about the work of schools.

Hargreaves and Fullan (1998) offer a set of guidelines for teachers for "getting out there" and committing to working with people in positive, forward-looking relationships, even when they may have misgivings or fears about the contact. We have adapted these guidelines to fit conversations about interpreting data and using the resulting insights to change programs and practices.

• *Make Students Partners.* Students' learning should be at the heart of everything that happens in schools. When students are engaged and involved in their learning, they learn more. When they see why they are doing something, they are more likely to participate. Students are also the most important points of connection between home and school. When students understand the school's priorities, there is more chance that the parents will hear about them as well.

- *Respond to Parents' Needs and Desires.* Parents give schools responsibility for providing the best care and education for their children. They deserve to be kept in the loop (and not just on Parents' Night) and even participate in decisions that affect their children. When schools and parents work together, they can pool important information that can complement and extend professional knowledge.

- *Become Assessment and Data Literate.* Conversations with parents are never comfortable if teachers feel exposed, vulnerable, or threatened. Teachers need to develop shared understanding about the evidence available to them (about the school and about individual students) so that they can explain their decisions and communicate about student learning clearly and confidently.

- *Don't Mind Your Own Business.* What happens outside the classroom can have profound effects on teachers and, more importantly, students. Moral courage requires risk taking and moving into both collaborative and confrontational relationships inside and outside schools to ensure that the teaching enterprise is fulfilling its mandate.

- *Use Emotional Intelligence.* Emotional intelligence allows teachers to step outside themselves, see their work from another angle, and understand other points of view as a way of creating more positive relationships with students, colleagues, parents, and others.

- *Help to Recreate Your Profession.* Teachers can influence the nature of a new professionalism in education by investing in their own learning and in the learning of others, including external constituents, as a valued and routine part of their work.

All of these activities draw students, parents, and teachers together in the kind of conversations that are challenging, informative, and productive, even when they are often emotional and unsettling.

Sharing Our Learning

Educators who have gone through a process of considering data have to remember that data do not speak for themselves. New audiences for the ideas also need to discuss the data, think about it, and see how the actions have emerged from the insights that the staff have gleaned. Sharing the information is as much a matter of understanding the audiences as managing the data. Knowledge of your audiences influences the nature of the display choices that you make in communicating the key messages. How much or how little will parents read? Should communication with the district administrators be in print or in person? Should you communicate to your audiences in pictures, words, or both? Where English is a second language, a picture may indeed say a thousand words. In other cases, studies have found parents to prefer written prose when receiving communication from their child's school or district.

There are a few basic rules for communicating about data. Results should be explained clearly and concisely, with no clutter or jargon. Your presentation of information should be self-explanatory and intuitive, chosen intentionally, with knowledge of purpose and audience in mind. For example, if you are going to use graphs, bar charts encourage comparison, so if you do not want to invite comparison, do not use a bar chart. Line graphs show progress over time. Pie charts are good for demographics.

Whatever approach you choose, make sure that the audience understands what you are trying to communicate. It is always a good idea to involve members of your audiences in the preparation and sharing of information to ensure that you are communicating in a way that makes sense to them. It also means that accountability conversations begin early in the process. It is rarely a linear journey but one that winds and bumps, requiring creativity and a willingness to take some chances.

Janet and Thomas were having coffee and struggling with the magnitude of the process that they had unleashed. Almost everyone in the school was on a team, and some people were on more than one. Then there was the School Improvement Team coordinating it all. Now they wanted to recruit people to be involved in sharing what they were learning with parents and others in the community. But they couldn't ask people to do any more.

They had already sent a newsletter home to parents announcing their literacy focus and the attention that they were going to pay to attendance. Janet had shared their process with the school council and invited them to participate on the planning teams.

She also knew that she had to send their plan to the district office and post their school improvement plan on the school's Web site. That was not a problem; she already had the art teacher working with a student who was interested in graphic design to take the concept maps and data summaries and action statements and turn them into displays for the Web page.

The action plans were in process and she would send them on to the district and post them on the Web site as well. She had written a detailed description of the process that they had gone through and was going to attach it to the report for the superintendent. She was even thinking about sending it to a principal's journal. It might be useful for someone else.

But she was still not happy. She wanted the work they were doing to come alive for people—to stimulate conversations, not at the district office but right here, in the school and the community so that they were all involved in making the school better. And she didn't know how to do it.

Thomas listened and made suggestions periodically, but he was stymied as well. Then he had an idea. Why not make a deal with the local cable TV station to do a series on adolescent literacy? The literacy team had already located some great video productions that they wanted to use with staff and the parent's council. Why not have them shown through cable, with opportunities for a phone-in question-and-answer period after each one to a panel of teachers? It didn't have to involve only H. C. Andersen. The teachers could come from all of the middle schools and high schools in the area. There could be follow-up with the schools to show what they are doing as well.

That was all Janet needed. She contacted the TV station and began negotiating for a series. And she asked the school council chair to come to the meeting at the TV station with her to talk about how they could involve parents, especially those who didn't speak English very well. By the end of the month, they were in motion. The cable TV company had a mandate to broadcast to the community about things that were directly relevant locally, and they were trying to make their programming more accessible to people who didn't speak English. If Janet would locate the programs to air and find parents from different language groups who would work with them to summarize the ideas from the programs, they would add summaries in various languages. They were ecstatic about an interactive panel, and they wanted to tape in the schools.

Janet knew this might be a tough idea to sell in the school at first, but she was convinced that it was worth it to show kids, their parents, and the community how important literacy was and how schools were working to ensure that all children had the language skills to be successful. She would see what she could do to move it along, slowly.

Assignment #14

Sharing the Learning

Sharing what you are learning is an integral part of the accountability conversation and, when it is all in place, one of the most rewarding. Getting there takes planning and time, however, always scarce resources. The first stage of sharing the learning may be very straightforward. Think about your audiences again. Who do you want to engage, and what information will be useful to them?

What are all the vehicles that you currently have available to communicate with your community, and how will you use them to communicate what you are doing?

Brainstorm other ways of engaging the audiences.

How will you bring key community members into the process? What can you do to start the conversations? How will you keep the conversations going?

Using Task Sheet #14 in the Resource section, go back to your earlier chart and fill in the key messages and mechanism for communicating with each group.

Sustaining the Process

The Cycle of Inquiry

I t should be very clear at this point that using data to make images of your school visible is not a one-shot process. It involves constant vigilance and sensitivity to issues that can help you think about what you are doing and target your energy where it will be most productive. The first picture gives you a starting point for action, but ongoing improvement requires regular attention to the state of affairs and to changes over time to ensure that your actions, decisions, and the allocation of resources reflect the school's values and priorities. As Louise Stoll (2004) says:

> "Real" school improvement comes from within and is about the ongoing and sustainable learning of pupils and all those inside and outside schools who care about pupil learning. (p. 6)

The challenge at hand is one of embedding and sustaining the capacities for using data wisely. Developing an inquiry habit of mind, becoming data literate, and creating a culture of inquiry are processes rather than singular events. And they are developmental processes, following a trajectory of sophistication by which competence unfolds at the individual level, in the perpetual refinement of that first painting, and in the expansion of images to a gallery full of paintings.

For individuals, as we have seen, the capacities are about learning and about conceptual change. The route is from emergent to proficient. In early stages, the capacities require deliberate cultivation. As competence grows, it becomes more automatic and familiar.

Stages in Growth From Novice to Expert

No practical experience. Dependent on rules.	Expects definitive answers. Some recognition of patterns. Limited experience. Still relies on rules.	Analytical. Locates and considers possible patterns. Has internalized the key dimensions so that they are automatic.	Uses analysis and synthesis. Sees the whole rather than aspects. Looks for links and patterns. Adjusts to adapt to the context.	Understands the context. Considers alternatives in an iterative way and integrates ideas into efficient solutions. Solves problems and makes ongoing adaptations automatically.

As is the case with expertise in all domains, proficiency comes from practice—"time-on-task" with built-in opportunities for corrective feedback. There are no shortcuts, quick fixes, or silver bullets. Practice is the route to automaticity. And automaticity—whether in the context of a child's reading performance or a school leader's use of data—is what supports the omnipresent and seemingly effortless character imbued in notions like "habit," "literacy," and "culture." And while some school staff are moving towards proficiency, others are beginning their journeys as emergent learners.

Using data to paint that first picture of your school in relation to a priority is not a linear process with a defined beginning, middle, and end. It is circular and iterative, as repeated passes lead to increased adjustment and refinement with the goal of a more honest representation, of a clearer image. What is at work here lies at the heart of what organizational psychologists refer to as a dynamic system. Dynamic systems have the following four central features in common: (a) a process that iterates routinely; (b) a process that has a feedback loop; (c) a context that includes internal constraints that shape the image; and (d) a context that sets external constraints that shape the actual organization that takes place (Katz, Sutherland, & Earl, 2002).

As an image of the first picture continues to sharpen, it also becomes clear that complex phenomena cannot be captured in a singular representation. Just as Monet did not try to represent his garden in a single image—he painted hundreds of representations of Giverny—using data to portray your school will require multiple paintings; in fact, a whole gallery full of paintings. Each painting will, of course, say something different as school improvement priorities are revisited, extended, and revised. The School Improvement Plan is not static; it is dynamic and organic. Although the messages in each image will be quite different as you begin the process again—setting the canvas, planning the picture, blocking the canvas, and so on—each will also clearly convey the story of its genesis by being inspired and shaped by those that were painted before.

It was October, again, and Thomas was on his way to H. C. Andersen for a meeting of the School Improvement Team and an initial review of the data that they had collected during September. As he drove, he reflected on what had happened over the last year. It had been pretty amazing, and he attributed much of the change to Janet's leadership. How many principals would have taken the risks that she had to look at data and then be so public about the problems that they were facing in the school? But it had worked. Most of the staff had jumped into the planning process. All of the teams were active, and the initial plans were being implemented. Trevor's team had moved into high gear almost immediately with the seventh-grade boys. They actually did individual profiles for every seventh-grade boy that showed them attendance patterns, test scores, areas of weakness on the informal reading and writing inventory, disciplinary incidents, family circumstances, areas of strength, and extracurricular activities. The team used a case-conference approach to review every one of the profiles and identified a group of 23 boys for intensive targeted intervention that included meeting with an adult mentor at the beginning and the end of every day to determine the areas for the student to work on that day and to review progress, using a planning diary to schedule additional help from subject teachers being trained to use different software packages designed to help them organize their thinking. And Dwayne had taken them on Friday afternoon field trips to apply their learning outside the school.

Sharon's team had all learned how to do the informal reading and writing assessment, and they had done it with the sixth-grade class the first week of school. They had also invited the language consultant from the district to offer a series of professional development sessions with the whole staff tailored to their plan, and more than half of the staff had taken the training, including a week-long institute in the summer. Janet rearranged the timetable so that the team could have a shared planning period, and they had spent the final term last year finding ways to embed literacy into all subject areas. At the same time, they had been developing an integrated approach to making comprehension and writing coherent activities from the student's perspective that crossed the subject boundaries.

The librarian, who was part of Sharon's team, had taken the books and articles that Janet had been collecting about adolescent literacy and was facilitating a study group who were meeting once a month to discuss possible ideas and debate their merits and relevance for H. C. Andersen.

The video series was still being organized, but they were moving ahead because it was very clear that the community was interested in literacy. The parent's council had coordinated the sixth-grade Parents' Night in June. It had been packed, and the parents were treated to a literacy fair full of examples of student work, discussion groups about adolescent literacy, and a huge display of books, magazines, and even comics with appeal for adolescent readers. The parent's council was determined to pursue the video series, and the chair was taking the lead.

In their meetings with the staff from Strathmere, the team with responsibility for creating a Transition Program and revamping the extracurricular activities decided to be bold. Instead of trying to offer a full-service extracurricular program at H. C. Andersen, they amalgamated the programs so that all of the H. C. Andersen students would participate in the extracurricular program at Strathmere, and the leaders of the programs from the two schools would share the load. This sharing became the first part of the Transition Program.

Although things seemed very positive on the surface, staffing had proven to be more complicated than Janet had imagined in the beginning. She had had private meetings with all the staff to get a sense of what the staff turnover might be, particularly with upcoming retirements. The surprise came when she actually talked with some of them. Three teachers indicated that they wanted to transfer to other schools. As one of them said, "I'm not really interested in being a literacy teacher. I teach science." The others felt that they would be happier in more traditional settings. There were also two teachers who were likely to retire in the next few years, Sharon being one of them. Janet hoped Sharon would stay for at least three years to get the program running. So, she had hired three new teachers, one of them right out of teacher's college to teach science and two others who were keen to come and be part of the H. C. Andersen approach.

The agenda for today's meeting contained two items. First was a review of the joint extracurricular program, and second, an initial look at of some new data describing students' ratings of their skills in literacy, student engagement in school and in their learning, and student perceptions of the value of schooling that the School Improvement Team had just collected through a survey of all of their students, done in the first week of school.

When Thomas arrived, the group was already assembled, and they were looking at the new data. He stood in the doorway and watched as they went through the interpretation questions that someone had posted on the wall. Then he joined the group and listened to the discussion.

- What is your initial interpretation of these data?
- What patterns seem to be meaningful? Why?
- What messages emerge from consideration of these data?
- What is still confusing or not clear?

Self-Rating of Skills(% saying excellent or very good)	6th Grade	7th Grade	8th Grade
Writing	62	66	60
Reading	79	76	73
Communication	86	80	75
Problem-solving	48	52	54
Computer	65	52	67

Hey, look at this. Most of the kids have a good image of their skills in reading, writing and communication, although we still have to watch the group that is now in Grade 8.

I think we should have a really close look at the ones who aren't confident and see who they are.

In fact, we should add this data to the profiles so that we can see how they view themselves in relation to the other things that we know about them.

It looks like problem solving may be an area that we need to concentrate on with the whole school. Let's put that idea into the mix for our discussion.

Student Engagement (% agree or strongly agree)	6th Grade	7th Grade	8th Grade
Student Engagement in the School			
I am really involved in this school.	42	52	56
I like to participate in school activities (e.g., sports, clubs, plays).	56	52	63
Involvement in Extracurricular Activities (% participating)			
Sports	38	40	38
Arts	12	18	20
Student government	12	18	13
Clubs	15	31	33
Student Engagement in Their Learning (% agree or strongly agree)			
I do more than the required work in my courses.	13	15	22
I participate actively in class discussions.	59	50	67
I pay attention to the teacher.	63	72	65
I like learning new things.	63	68	66
I am interested in what I am learning in class.	41	48	48

(Continued)

Student Engagement (% agree or strongly agree)	6th Grade	7th Grade	8th Grade
I complete my assignments.	76	68	59
When school work is very difficult, I stop trying.	17	16	13
I do as little work as possible; I just want to get by.	16	12	13
I get so interested in something at school (like an idea or an activity) that I keep working on it outside of school.	9	32	21
I skipped class (more than once a month).	42	48	49
Time Spent on Homework (% indicating)	1	0	2
None	10	14	7
Less than 1 hour/week	52	34	35
1–3 hours	23	40	39
4–7 hours	10	4	16
8–14 hours	3	8	0
15+ hours			
School is one of the most important things in my life.	69	84	70
What I take in school is relevant to my life.	58	60	62
Most of the time, I'd like to be any place other than in school.	35	40	42
School is more important than most people think.	77	80	85
Most of what I learn in school will be useful when I get a job.	68	52	60
School is often a waste of time.	38	40	44
Most of the things we learn in class are useless.	34	28	51

This is worrisome. Only about half of the students say that they are really involved in the school.

At least the eighth graders are the most engaged.

If we look at extracurricular, there is a pattern here. Sports and clubs are the highest. That's what we would expect. But only half say that they like to participate.

Fewer sixth graders are involved. Do they even know what the extracurricular program is about? We've talked it up for the others, but maybe we didn't for them.

I wonder how many kids participate in at least something. Could we ask Jason to do an analysis to tell us that?

The homework time is interesting. Most are doing at least one hour a week—I should hope so. But some are doing over eight. Is that reasonable?

I'd really like to spend some time looking at the results from student engagement in their learning. It seems to me that there may be a pattern of less engagement for the younger kids. And maybe we need to focus on persistence for all of them. Can we put some time aside to really think about what this means?

Value of Schooling	6th Grade	7th Grade	8th Grade
School is one of the most important things in my life.	69	84	70
What I take in school is relevant to my life.	58	60	62
Most of the time, I'd like to be any place other than in school.	35	40	42
School is more important than most people think.	77	80	85
Most of what I learn in school will be useful when I get a job.	68	52	60
School is often a waste of time.	38	40	44
Most of the things we learn in class are useless.	34	28	51

I find this reassuring. They think that school is important, even if they don't like being here. That gives us something to build on.

For sure, we're going to make it so relevant and engaging that they will be clamoring to get it.

At this stage, Thomas suggested that they talk about the joint extracurricular program and then think about how they were going to discuss it and the new information with the staff, and position their discussion in the School Improvement Plan.

THE NEXT PICTURE, AND THE NEXT, AND THE NEXT

When schools get engaged in a cycle of inquiry and have routine account-ability conversations, they find themselves examining their practices with each other and with the broader community—explicitly, publicly, and col-lectively. This is not a linear process with formal reporting events but is ongoing, nonlinear and iterative, involving reflection, action, and com-munication. Once it starts, any of the activities can be revisited at any time. The School Improvement Plan becomes a living process, with the team collecting, evaluating, and disseminating information all of the time to monitor their progress and revisit their priorities.

We can imagine a time when schools will be the pillars of a "learning society," where

- there will be a convergence of policy and practice to promote continual learning, reflection, and change, based on careful atten-tion to evidence combined with insight, professional knowledge, and common sense;
- all school leaders will have well-developed inquiry habits of mind, be confidently data literate, and be happily working in and promot-ing cultures of inquiry in their schools; and
- legislated reform does not hold school leaders accountable just for the results that are achieved by their students but also expects them to use internally and externally generated data to routinely investi-gate, reflect on, adapt, and improve programs.

School leaders would meet this kind of accountability by showing how they and their staff use high-quality data to identify strengths and weaknesses in the program, make changes, evaluate the impact of the changes, and make adjustments (and sometimes even major changes in direction) as a result of what they learn from the data that they consider.

Over time, schools will each develop a public gallery full of paintings, painted by many different artists and representing many facets of school life, all of them founded on evidence, on interpretation and on careful judgments, and all of them open to appraisal and reaction from outside.

Resource

Task Sheets for Assignments

TASK SHEET #1

Our School

List of descriptors submitted by staff members:

Composite description that everyone agrees about:

Areas of disagreement or uncertainty:

TASK SHEET #2

What Are the Accountability Requirements in Your Context?

What does "accountability" mean to you?

- National:

- State/province:

- District:

What do you currently do to satisfy these requirements?

(Continued)

What data are you expected to use?

Who reviews your accountability reports, and what feedback do you get?

What could accountability mean, and how might it change your practices?

TASK SHEET #3

Self-Assessment of Capacity for Leading in a Data-Rich World

Put a 0, 1, 2, or 3 beside each of the capacities using this scale:

3 = I've got this one sorted. I feel very competent and confident about my capacity here.

2 = I probably need a little work here, just to brush up and feel competent.

1 = I think I know what this means, but I'm not sure if I have it.

0 = This is new to me. Never even thought about it.

Inquiry Habit of Mind	
Reserve judgment and have a tolerance for ambiguity	
Value deep understanding	
Take a range of perspectives and systematically pose increasingly focused questions	
Data Literate	
Think about purpose(s)	
Recognize sound and unsound	
Knowledgeable about statistical and measurement concepts	
Recognize other kinds of data	
Make interpretation paramount	
Pay attention to reporting and to audiences	
A Culture of Inquiry in the School Community	
Involve others in interpreting and engaging with the data	
Stimulate an internal sense of "urgency"	
Make time	
Use "critical friends"	

TASK SHEET #4

Purpose, Context

Issues identified by the staff, with their rationales, grouped into categories:

Category of Issue	Rationale

Top three issues:

Who has responsibility for each "needs assessment"?

TASK SHEET #5

Identifying Audiences

Put the names and positions of all of the people currently involved in the planning in the boxes. Add the names of everyone who needs to be involved but are not currently in the circles.

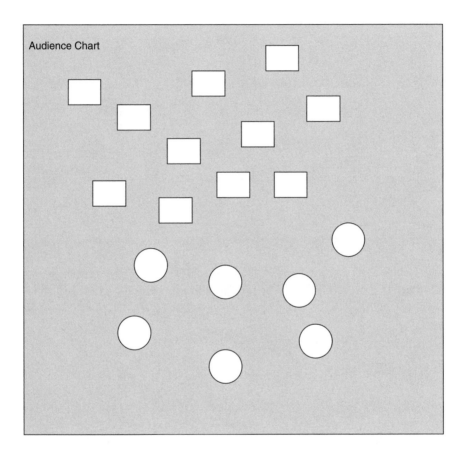

Audience Chart

TASK SHEET #6

Charting Your Futures

Area for attention: _____

Brainstormed list of possible futures:

Concept map:

What will the probable future be for this school? Why do you think this?

Where would we like to go? Create a detailed scenario that describes the future as you prefer it to be:

TASK SHEET #7

Initial Environmental Scan

Top three priorities:

What do you know already? What data do you have that informs you about your priorities?

How could you find out more?

What did you learn from locating or collecting additional data?

TASK SHEET #8

Selecting Your Colors (Indicator Categories)

Priority: _____

What do you think is going on in relation to your priority? How would you explain the situation?

What do you already know about each indicator category in relation to your priority?

What additional information do you need (considering each category) in order to examine your hypotheses?

TASK SHEET #9

From Indicator Categories to Data Sources

Indicator category (color): _____

Questions	Data Sources, Types, and Access Procedures

Actual data sources located:

TASK SHEET #10

A Quality Guide

Data source: _____

How much confidence do you have in these data? What cautions should you take in interpretation?

What reference points can you use for interpretation?

Does the data give you information about the things you want to understand?

(Continued)

Is there enough detail to guide your thinking?

What are the limitations of these data?

TASK SHEET #11

A Guide to Interpretation

Data source: _____

What is your initial interpretation of these data? What patterns seem to be meaningful? Why?

What is confusing or not clear?

What other information might help you in your interpretation?

How might your interpretations change with additional information?

What messages do you have to share from consideration of these data?

Concept map that includes all of the interpretations together:

TASK SHEET #12

Consensus About Interpretations

What have you learned from the data and the interpretation exercise that everyone agrees needs immediate attention?

What are important insights that deserve attention?

What are the areas that you need to know more about?

TASK SHEET #13

Moving to Action

Action statement: _____

Who is Team Leader?

Who are the Team Members?

What are the detailed tasks to make this action statement into real action?

Who will do what?

What are the timelines and milestones?

What resources do people need?

How will you monitor progress and ensure coherence?

What indicator categories will you need to use?

TASK SHEET #14

Sharing the Learning

Who is already involved? Who do you want to have involved?

What are all the vehicles that you currently have available to communicate with your community, and how will you use them to communicate what you are doing with each of your audiences?

How will you bring key community members into the process? What can you do to start the conversations? How will you keep the conversations going?

References

Abelson, R. (1995). *Statistics as principled argument.* Hillsdale, NJ: Lawerence Erlbaum Associates.

Allen, R. (Ed.) (1991). *Oxford English dictionary.* New York: Oxford University Press

Argyris, C., & Schön, D. (1978). *Organizational learning: A theory of action perspective.* Reading, MA.: Addison-Wesley.

Barber, M. (2001). *From good to great: Large-scale reform in England.* Paper presented at Futures of Education conference, Zurich, Switzerland.

Barth, R. (2001). *Learning by heart.* San Francisco: Jossey Bass.

Beare, H. (2001). *Creating the future school.* London: Routledge Falmer.

Connelly, M., & Clandinin, J. (1988). *Teachers as curriculum planners: Narratives of experience.* NY: Teachers College Press.

Costa, A. L., & Kallick, B. (1995). Through the lens of a critical friend. In A. L. Costa & B. Kallick (Eds.), *Assessment in the learning organization: Shifting the paradigm* (pp. 153–156). Alexandria VA: Association for Supervision and Curriculum Development.

Costa, A., & Kallick, B. (2000). *Discovering and exploring habits of mind.* Alexandria, VA: Association for Supervision and Curriculum Development.

Darling-Hammond, L. (1994). Performance-based assessment and educational equity. *Harvard Educational Review 64*(1), 5–30.

Darling-Hammond, L. (2004). Standards, accountability, and school reform. *Teachers College Record , 106,* 1047–1085.

Donovan, M. S., Bransford, J., & Pellegrino, J. (Eds.) (1999). *How people learn: Bringing research and practice.* Washington, DC: National Academy Press.

Earl, L. (1998). Developing indicators: The call for accountability. *Policy Options,* July-August, 20–24.

Earl, L., & Katz, S. (2002). Leading schools in a data rich world. In K. Leithwood, P. Hallinger, G. Furman, P. Gronn, J. MacBeath, B. Mulford & K. Riley (Eds.) The second international handbook of educational leadership and administration. Dordrecht, Netherlands: Kluwer.

Earl, L., & Lee, L. (1998). *The evaluation of the Manitoba School Improvement Program.* Toronto, Canada: Walter and Duncan Gordon Foundation.

Earl, L., & LeMahieu, P. (1997). Rethinking assessment and accountability. In A. Hargreaves (Ed.), *Rethinking educational change with heart and mind* (149–168). *1997 ASCD Yearbook.* Alexandria, VA: Association for Supervision and Curriculum Development.

Earl, L., Watson, N., Levin, B., Leithwood, K., Fullan, M., & Torrance, N. (2003). Final report of the external evaluation of England's national literacy and numeracy strategies. Final report. Watching & learning 3. England: Department for Education and Skills (DfES).

Education Commission of the States (2000). *Informing practices and improving results with data-driven decisions.* ECS Issue Paper retrieved September 9. 2004, from www.ecs.org.

Education Quality and Accountability Office (2002). *EQAO annual report.* Ontario Government Printer.

Ennis, Robert H. (1996). *Critical thinking.* Upper Saddle River, NJ: Prentice-Hall.

Firestone, W., Mayrowetz, D., & Fairman, J. (1998). Performance-based assessment and instructional change: The effects of testing in Maine and Maryland. *Educational Evaluation and Policy Analysis, 20* (2), 95–113.

Fullan, M. (1999). *Change forces: The sequel.* London: Falmer.

Fullan, M. (2001). *Leading in a culture of change.* San Francisco: Jossey-Bass.

Gray, J., Hopkins, D., Reynolds, D., Wilcox, B., Farrell, S., & Jesson, D. (1999). *Improving schools: Performance and potential.* Buckingham, England: Open University Press.

Hannay, L. M., Mahony, M., & MacFarlane, N. (2004). Reconstructing professional learning. Paper presented at the British Educational Leadership and Management Association Research Conference, Oxford University.

Hargreaves, A., Earl, L., & Schmidt, M. (2002). Four perspectives on classroom assessment reform. *American Educational Research Journal, 39,* 69–100.

Hargreaves, A., & Fullan, M. (1998). *What's worth fighting for out there.* Buckingham, England: Open University Press.

Herman, J., & Gribbons, B. (2001). *Lessons learned in using data to support school inquiry and continuous improvement: Final report to the Stuart Foundation.* Los Angeles, CA: University of California Center for the Study of Evaluation (CSE).

Hord, S. (1997). Professional learning communities: Communities of continuous inquiry and improvement. Austin, TX, Southwest Educational Development Laboratory.

Jaeger, R., Gorne, B., Johnson, R., Putnam, S., & Williamson, G. (1993). *Designing and developing effective school report cards: A research synthesis.* Center for Educational Research and Evaluation. Chapel Hill: University of North Carolina.

Katz, S., Sutherland, S., & Earl, L. (2002). Developing an evaluation habit of mind. *The Canadian Journal of Program Evaluation, 17*(2), 103–119.

Katz, S., Sutherland, S., & Earl, L. (in press). Towards an evaluation habit of mind: Plotting the trajectory. *Teachers College Record.*

Katzenmeyer, M., & Moller, G. (2000). Awakening the sleeping giant: Helping teachers develop as leaders. Thousand Oaks, CA: Corwin.

Keating, D. (1996). Habits of mind for a learning society: Educating for human development. In. D. Olson & N. Torrance (Eds.), *The handbook of education and human development* (pp. 461–481). Cambridge, MA: Blackwell.

Leithwood, K., Edge, K., & Jantzi, D. (1999). Educational accountability: The state of the art. Gutersloh, Germany: Bertelsmann Foundation Publishers.

Love, N. (2000). *Using data—Getting results: Collaborative inquiry for school-based mathematics and science reform.* Cambridge, MA: Regional Alliance for Mathematics and Science Education Reform at MERC.

MacBeath, J. (1998). 'I didn't know he was ill': The role and value of the critical friend, in L. Stoll & K. Myers (Eds.), *No quick fixes: Perspectives on schools in difficulty*. London: Falmer Press.

McNamara, J., & Thompson, D. (n.d.) Teaching statistics in principal preparation programs: Part 1. Commerce: Research Department, Texas A&M University.

Mitchell, C., & Sackney, L. (2000). *Profound improvement: Building capacity for a learning community*. Lisse, The Netherlands: Swets & Zeitlinger.

O'Connor, J., & McDermott, I. (1997). *The art of systems thinking*. London: Thorsons.

Putnam, R., & Borko, H. (1997). Teacher learning: Implications of new views of cognition. In B. J. Biddle, T. L. Good, & I. F. Goodson (Eds.), *The international handbook of teachers* (pp. 1223–1296). Dordrecht, The Netherlands: Kluwer.

Rosenholtz, S. J. (1989). *Teachers' workplace: The social organization of schools*. New York: Teachers College Press.

Senge, P. M. (1990). *The fifth discipline: The art and practice of the learning organization*. London: Century Business.

Stoll, L. (2004). *Networked learning communities as professional learning communities*. Paper Commissioned by Aporia Consulting Ltd.

Stoll, L., & Fink, D. (1996). *Changing our schools: Linking school effectiveness and school improvement*. Buckingham, England: Open University Press.

Stoll, L., Fink, D., & Earl, L. (2003). *It's about learning and it's about time: What's in it for schools*. London, Falmer.

Supovitz, J., & Klein, V. (2003). *Mapping a course for improved student learning: How innovative schools systematically use student performance data to guide improvement*. Philadelphia, PA: Consortium for Policy Research in Education.

Sykes, G. (1999). Teacher and student learning: Strengthening their connection. In L. Darling-Hammond & G. Sykes (Eds.), *Teaching as the learning profession: Handbook of policy and practice* (pp. 151–179). San Francisco, CA: Jossey-Bass.

Whitty, G., Power, S., & Halpin, D. (1998). *Devolution and choice in education: The school, the state and the market*. Buckingham, England: Open University Press.

Index

Abelson, R., 63
Accountability
  defining, 9–12
  educational change and, 10
  role of data in, 2–3
  task sheets, 111–112
  through informed professional
    judgment, 10–12
Acting on data interpretations,
  93–96, 124
Argyris, C., 6
Assessment data, 53–54, 59–60
  informal reading and writing, 61–62
  interpretation of, 66–72
Attendance data, 60
  interpretation of, 72–76
Audiences, 34–36
  engaged in data interpretations, 97–98
  identifying, 115

Barber, Michael, 10–11
Barth, R., 63
Beare, H., 37
Beliefs about data, 7–9

Change
  accountability and, 10
  using data to take charge of, 14–15
Common uses of data, 13–14
Community surveys of needs, 61
  interpretation of, 72–76
Conceptual change, 8
Consensus about interpretation of data,
  87–92, 123
Costa, A. L., 21, 26, 54
Critical friends, 21–22, 54–56
Cultures of inquiry, 20–22, 28–29
  consensus about interpretation in,
    87–92
  engaging and sharing in, 96–100

sustaining, 101–108
taking action in, 92–96

Darling-Hammond, Linda, 7, 10
Data
  accountability and, 2–3
  assessment, 53–54, 59–60, 66–72
  attendance, 60, 72–76
  based decision making, 4–5, 29–30
  common uses of, 13–14
  educators' skepticism about, 3–5
  engaging audiences in, 97–98
  fear of evaluation and, 4
  home language, 60, 72–76
  identifying needed, 52–56
  indicator categories, 49–51
  interpretation, 20–21, 63–86,
    122, 123
  literacy, 18–20, 27–28, 45–86, 98
  mistrust of, 3–4
  need for, 5–7
  as a policy lever, 2–3
  priorities, 46–52
  purpose and context of, 19, 31–32, 33,
    47, 114
  quality of, 56–63, 120–121
  recognizing other kinds of, 19
  recognizing sound and unsound, 19
  role in informed professional judgment,
    12–14
  sharing, 98–100, 125
  sources, 58–59, 119
  technology advances and, 1–2
  thinking differently about, 7–9
  urgency of, 21
  used for taking charge of change,
    14–15
Decision making, data-based, 4–5, 29–30
  audiences, 34–36, 97–98, 115
  critical friends and, 21–22, 54–56

inquiry habit of mind and, 18, 26–27
planing in, 36–44
purpose and context of, 31–32,
   33, 47, 114
roles in, 32–34

Earl, Lorna M., 7, 8, 10, 12, 35
Educators and leaders. *See also* Leadership
   becoming active players in data-rich
      environment, 6–7
   beliefs about data, 7–9
   creating a culture of inquiry, 20–22,
      28–29, 87–100
   critical friends, 21–22, 54–56
   data-literate, 18–20
   emotional intelligence, 98
   fear of data and evaluation, 4
   informed professional judgment of,
      10–14
   inquiry habit of mind in, 18,
      26–27, 31–44
   lack of training in data-based decision
      making, 4–5
   leading in a data-rich world, 22
   mistrust of data, 3–4
   professional resources, 62–63
   self-assessment, 113
   sustaining a culture of inquiry,
      101–108
Emotional intelligence, 98
Engaging the audiences, 97–98
Ennis, Robert H., 63
Evaluation and data, 4
Every Child Matters (UK), 7

Fear of data and evaluation, 4
Friends, critical, 21–22, 54–56
Fullan, M., 21, 26, 35, 47, 97
Futures
   possible, 37–38, 41
   preferable, 40–44, 41–42
   probable, 38–39, 41
   vision and planning, 36–37, 116

Gribbons, B., 5

Hargreaves, A., 47, 97
Herman, J., 5
Home language data, 60
   interpretation of, 72–76
Hord, S., 28

Indicator categories, 49–51, 118–119
Information age, the, 2

Informed professional judgment
   accountability through, 10–12
   role of data in, 12–14
   skills needed in, 17
Initial environmental scans,
   43–44, 117
Inquiry habit of mind, 18, 26–27, 31–44
   purpose and context in, 31–32, 33
   roles in, 32–34
Interpretation of data, 20–21, 63, 84–86
   acting on, 93–96, 124
   on attendance, 72–76
   from community surveys, 72–76
   consensus about, 87–92, 123
   guide to, 86, 122
   on language in the home, 72–76
   from reading and writing assessments,
      76–80
   sharing, 98–100, 125
   from state literacy assessments, 66–72
   success in secondary school, 80–85
   time required for, 21, 64–66

Jaeger, R., 20

Kallick, B., 21, 26, 54
Katz, Steven, 7, 8
Katzenmeyer, M., 32
Klein, V., 53

Language, home, 60, 72–76
Leadership
   culture of inquiry and, 20–22, 28–29,
      87–100
   in a data-rich world, 22, 113
   painting metaphor for, 23–25
   stages of growth and sustaining,
      101–108
Leithwood, K., 35
LeMahieu, P., 10
Levin, B., 35
Literacy, data, 18–20, 27–28,
      45–46, 98
   asking the right questions and, 46–52
   assessments and, 59–63
   data quality and, 56–59
   determining what data is needed and,
      52–56
   identifying what we want to know and,
      46–52
   indicator categories and, 49–51,
      118–119
   professional resources, 62–63
Love, N., 63

McNamara, J., 5
Measurement and statistical concepts, 19
Mistrust of data, 3–4
Moller, G., 32

Necessity of data, 5–7
No Child Left Behind (NCLB) legislation,
    3, 7

Painting as a metaphor for leadership,
    23–25
Parents, responding to, 98
Planning
    action, 93–96
    initial environmental scans in,
        43–44, 117
    possible futures in, 37–38, 41
    preferable futures in, 40–44, 41–42
    probable futures in, 38–39, 41
    vision of future in, 36–37, 116
Policy decisions and data, 2–3, 7, 15
Possible futures, 37–38, 41
Preferable futures, 40–44, 41–42
Priorities, setting information, 46–52
Probable futures, 38–39, 41
Professional resources, 62–63
Purpose and context, 19,
    31–32, 33, 47, 114

Quality of data
    assessments, 59–62
    guide to, 120–121
    judging, 56–57
    professional resources
        and, 62–63
    reference points and, 57–58
    reliability and, 57
    sources and, 58–59
    validity and, 57

Reading and writing
    assessments, 61–62
    interpretation of, 76–80
Reference points, data, 57–58
Reliability of data, 57
Roles in data use, 32–34, 33

Schön, D., 6
Secondary school, student success in,
    80–85
Self-assessment of capacity
    for leading, 113
Senge, P. M., 18
Sharing information, 98–100, 125
Skepticism about data, 3–5
Sound versus unsound data, 19
Sources, data, 58–59, 119
Statistical and measurement
    concepts, 19
Stoll, Louise, 101
Students
    as partners in data, 97–98
    performance data, 53–54, 59–60
    reading and writing assessments,
        61–62, 76–80
    success in secondary school, 80–85
    testing, 2–3
Supovitz, J., 53
Surveys, community, 61
Sustaining cultures of
    inquiry, 101–108
Sutherland, S., 7, 8

Task sheets
    accountability, 111–112
    school profile, 110
Testing, student, 2–3
Theory of action in reform policy
    agendas, 7
Thompson, D., 5
Time required for data interpretation, 21,
    64–66
Torrance, N., 35
Training, data-based decision making,
    4–5

Unsound data, 19
Urgency of data, 21

Validity of data, 57
Vision of future, 36–37

Watson, N., 35

**CORWIN
PRESS**

The Corwin Press logo—a raven striding across an open book—represents the union of courage and learning. Corwin Press is committed to improving education for all learners by publishing books and other professional development resources for those serving the field of PreK–12 education. By providing practical, hands-on materials, Corwin Press continues to carry out the promise of its motto: **"Helping Educators Do Their Work Better."**